CHOOSING TO CHEAT

Who Wins When Family and Work Collide?

A N D Y   S T A N L E Y

THOMAS NELSON PUBLISHERS®
Nashville

A Division of Thomas Nelson, Inc.
www.ThomasNelson.com

Published in Nashville, Tennessee, by Thomas Nelson, Inc.

Library of Congress Control Number: 2002109112
ISBN: 0-7852-6524-4

Printed in the United States of America

2 3 4 5 BVG 05 04 03 02

FOR BOB WALKER,

Father of my wife
Grandfather of my children
Example to me

CONTENTS

FOREWORD

Last year my wife, Margaret, and I were having dinner with Andy Stanley and his wife, Sandra, as he shared with us his vision for our church. It was a pivotal moment for the leaders and congregation of North Point Community Church, because we had once again outgrown our space. Andy was already preaching twice on Sunday, and it had been suggested that the church start a Saturday night service. As he shared with us that night his hesitation about cutting into his family time on Saturdays, I once again saw the heart and wisdom of this godly man.

Week after week, using the Bible as his guide, Andy teaches and confronts his congregation with the important challenges we all face. One of those challenges is finding a balance between work and family responsibilities. And in this book, *Choosing to Cheat: Who Wins When Family and Work Collide?*, he eloquently addresses the issue. He asks us: Is there a more important subject than this? Andy believes that for leaders, professionals in all industries, pastors, teachers, homemakers, and parents the issue is the same—we have a critical need to bring balance to our lives.

Andy asks the tough questions and then gives us some answers about how we can go about accomplishing what may be life's greatest challenge—achieving our goals outside the home when faced with the crucial task of partnering and parenting at home. How can we be successful without sacrificing our relationship with those closest to us?

Andy's answers are biblical, practical, and extremely relevant to our modern way of life. He does not pull any punches. He confronts us with truth and transparency. Just as he had made a commitment in his own life to balance his family time with his work, he encourages us to make similar commitments.

This is a life-changing book. And I think one of the main reasons it is life-changing is because a godly man who makes choices in his own life to never sacrifice his family for success has written it. If he wins the world but loses his family, what has he gained?

Every couple, every parent, and every leader needs to read this book and consider the question: Who wins when my family and work collide?

DR. JOHN C. MAXWELL
Founder, The INJOY Group
Bestselling author of *The 21 Irrefutable*
Laws of Leadership

INTRODUCTION

When I suggested *Choosing to Cheat* as the title for this book, I was warned that the connotations associated with the term *cheat* may scare people off. So the fact that you have chosen to pick this book up and read it is an indication that you are a person of profound courage. For almost everyone, the word *cheating* has negative connotations, especially if you've ever been cheated. Students cheat in school. Adults cheat on their income taxes. Husbands cheat on their wives. Most of us have cheated in a card game or two.

So why the title?

When we cheat, we choose to give up one thing in hopes of gaining something else of greater value. Typically, this involves giving up an intangible virtue for a tangible reward. Students give up their integrity for the sake of a grade. Salesmen trade their credibility for the sake of a sale. Every April, we are tempted to cash in our honesty for the sake of a few dollars.

So when I talk about "choosing to cheat," I'm referring to the decision to give up one thing in order to gain something else. This is something we do every day. We don't think of it as cheating. Especially when we are making what most people would consider a *good* trade. Saying no to dessert for the sake of one's waistline would hardly be considered cheating. But isn't it true that when you say no to dessert, you have cheated your appetite? Both your appetite and your self-control cry out for your attention. To say *yes* to one is to say *no* to the other. Either your appetite or your self-control is going to be cheated out of what it demands. You can't have it both ways.

In light of this broader application of the term *cheating*, you are a cheater. Daily you make decisions to give up one thing in order to gain something else. This is especially true within the arena of your schedule. You face a variety of responsibilities and opportunities: work… family… hobbies… clubs… leagues… the list is endless. Each competes for your attention. Each competes for your most valuable resource, your time.

But to give each of these the time it demands or deserves would require more time than you have. So you cheat. You give up certain opportunities for the sake of others. You invest in some relationships, while neglecting others. You allocate your time the best that you can, knowing all the while that somebody is going to feel cheated. Unfortunately, that "somebody" is usually someone we care a great deal about.

And that brings us to the point of this little book.

I have spent hundreds of hours with men and women who have cheated their families for the sake of their career goals. They all admitted knowing there was a problem. They all tried in their own way to dissipate the tension. But they felt trapped. Over time they dreaded coming home. The reception was cold. The conversation was filled with sarcasm used to hide the pain. The discomforts of home drove many to work even longer hours. Others went to the gym. Some to the bar. A few found comfort in the arms of a co-worker or friend.

Eventually things unraveled to the point that they had no choice but to seek help. For most, there was an event, "a wake-up call." *Suddenly*, their kids had withdrawn. *Overnight,* someone's grades had dropped off. *Out of nowhere,* she was more interested in tennis than the family. *Without explanation,* intimacy evaporated. But in each case, these were symptoms of something that had been brewing for quite some time.

This is not a struggle relegated to some diminutive segment of society. We all wrestle with the tension between work and family. Regardless of which side of the equation you are on, you know what it is like to deal with the endless cycle of guilt, anger, jealousy, and rejection. Whether you are the one trying to get home or the partner left waiting at home the feelings are pretty much the same. And left unattended, these seething emotions have the potential to erode the foundation of even the strongest marriages.

But there is a solution. Strangely enough, the solution is similar to the problem. Both involve cheating. Simply put, you must choose to cheat at work rather than at home.

In Chapter 1, you will be introduced to some friends of mine. Their struggle typifies the experiences of many. In Chapters 2 through 5, we will focus on the dynamic created in the heart of a spouse or child who feels cheated. In Section 2, we will develop a strategy for change. The principles in these final chapters are drawn largely from the life of a young man who found himself with a dilemma similar to ours. The primary difference being that his life, not merely his livelihood, was on the line.

Choosing to Cheat is about establishing priorities. A priority is something you put ahead of something else. A priority is something you say *yes* to even when it means saying *no* to other important things. Everybody cheats. This principle is already at work in your life… one way or another. When you put it to work *for* you, it has the power to transform every facet of your life. When we choose to cheat in accordance with God's priorities for our lives, it is an invitation for Him to bless us in ways we never dared to imagine.

SECTION 1

Is Cheating the Problem?

1

⌒

EVERYBODY CHEATS

Bill entered the work force with all the subtlety of the space shuttle entering the earth's orbit. With an MBA from Harvard and tremendous leadership instincts, it seemed his destiny to move from one accomplishment to the next.

Growing up, Bill had watched his father work sunup to sundown plowing fields, mowing lawns, and working in a factory. But somehow the family never seemed to get ahead. With the opportunities Bill had been given to make a better life, he felt a responsibility before God to be a good steward of those prospects. In essence, he felt called by God to achieve his maximum career potential as a servant-leader in business.

And achieve he did.

Upon graduating from Harvard, Bill was offered his dream job—he was one of the first four people hired for a new General Motors startup soon to be known as Saturn. The Japanese dominated the current small-car market, and GM had ambitious goals of competing against them. It took seven years to prepare for the launch. But when the first Saturn rolled off the assembly line, the American car market would never be the same.

Fueled by that early success, Bill moved up quickly through the GM ranks. His skills, gifts, and work ethic made him perfectly suited for high-level executive leadership. He was destined for the top. At the age of thirty-four, he received an incredible offer to become the president of Saab Cars, USA. So he left GM to take on a whole new level of demands. Bill excelled in his new position and was soon put in charge of Saab in Asia, South America, and Canada as well. There seemed to be no limit to his future, but at the same time there seemed to be no end to his frustration.

You see, career wasn't the only arena in which Bill had goals for his life. He and his wife, Carol, had dreams for their family as well. By the time Bill reached his peak at Saab, they had three daughters. While each of Bill's promotions took them a step closer to reaching their financial goals, each demanded more of his time as well. Time that he knew belonged to Carol and the kids.

Carol embraced her role with the same tenacity Bill exhibited in the marketplace. She was committed to being a team player. She didn't always like the hand she was dealt, but she accepted it and did the best she could. She held down the homefront while Bill worked to build a bright future for the family. But there was always the frustration, the loneliness, and at times, the anger.

As Bill describes it, "I was traveling more than 50 percent of the time. There were car shows and dealer meetings all the time. And when I was home, I wasn't really there—I had a late-night conference call with Japan, or an early morning conference call with Sweden. In my heart, I wanted to be with my family. But I felt like this job was something I had to do. Our family had financial goals, and I felt like God had given me this talent that I should be using. And I viewed each promotion as His reward for a job well done. The truth is, I just couldn't say no. Looking back, it wasn't God prying me away from my family. It was me."

One day, a close friend called Carol to wish her happy birthday. During their casual conversation, a wave of emotions began to surface, surprising even Carol. It was the third year in a row that Bill had been out of town on her birthday. He hadn't forgotten. He just had a job to do. And she had willingly agreed he should go. But somehow, in that moment, Carol was hit with the reality that the very things they were working so hard to achieve were slipping through their fingers with each passing day.

In the weeks that followed, Bill and Carol had many heart-to-heart conversations. Carol shared that the life they were living simply wasn't what she had signed up for. As Bill began to notice the despair in her countenance, he knew he had to make some major changes. Fast.

"I looked at Carol and she was bawling her eyes out," he explains. "I knew that if I continued down this path, I was going to lose my family."

Bill made a decision right then and there. He didn't have a

plan. He wasn't sure how he could pull off the changes necessary to bring balance to his personal life. He didn't know how he could disentangle himself from his involvement in the car industry. But one thing was certain: He refused to keep going in the direction he was going. The remarkable events that followed marked Bill for the rest of his life. As he and Carol describe it, the aftermath of Bill's decision to reorder his world is the clearest indication of God's presence in their lives and marriage as anything they had experienced.

FORCED TO CHEAT

In the midst of their crisis, Bill and Carol heard me share a simple principle that serves as the thesis of this book. On the occasion Bill and Carol heard me share this simple truth, it was the first time I had ever shared it publicly. I had been sharing this principle with couples for more than a decade in the privacy of a counseling environment. But for some reason, I never considered the value of sharing this principle in a group setting. Since that time I have had the opportunity to share this principle with thousands of business and church leaders, and the response has been overwhelming.

Perhaps the reason I was initially reluctant to talk about this in public is that it highlights a tension I live with every day. This is not a lesson I have learned and put behind me. This is a principle I have to make a conscious decision to apply daily, or it will slip away. Like many people I know, I love what I do. I rarely have a bad day at the office. My work environment could not be any better suited for my gifts and person- ality. I love to go to work. And like you, I have more to do than I can ever hope to get done. Every afternoon when I leave the office there are loose ends. Phone calls that didn't get returned. Meetings that had to be cut short. People who need and deserve my undivided attention.

At the same time, I love my wife and kids. I love to go home. And like you, there is more to do at home than will ever get done. Never once have my kids looked at me and said, "Hey Dad, we've played enough. Why don't you run back in the house and see if you can get some work done." Never once has Sandra complained about me coming home too early or doing too many things to help her at home.

What it boils down to is this: Someone is going to get cheated. Worse yet, somebody is going to *feel* cheated. Somebody is going to feel as if I am not giving them what they deserve or need. The issue is never, "Am I cheating?" The issue is always, "Where am I cheating?" Or, "Where am I choosing to cheat?"

WHERE ARE YOU CHEATING?

Everybody cheats. We have to. You have several important calls on your life. You have career potential to fulfill, a spouse to love, a family to raise, a ministry to perform. The list goes on. Each of these things has tremendous merit in your life and for the world at large. None of them should be neglected.

However, when you consider the limited number of hours

in a day, there's no way you can reach your full potential in all of those areas. There's just not enough time.

Your situation isn't that different from mine. If you stayed at work until everything was finished . . . if you took advantage of every opportunity that came your way . . . if you sought out every angle to maximize your abilities, improve your skills, and advance your career . . . you would never go home.

Likewise, if you stayed at home until every ounce of affection was poured out in all the appropriate places . . . if you kept giving until every emotional need was met . . . if you did every chore, finished the "honey do" list, and did everything necessary to ensure that everyone felt loved . . . you would never make it to work.

In fact, if you are a parent, you know that your kids alone could command every waking hour if you let them. Add to that your fitness goals, hobbies, and friendships. The list is endless and so are the time requirements.

So let me take some pressure off you. Your problem is not discipline. Your problem is not organization. Your problem is not that you have yet to stumble onto the perfect schedule. And your problem is not that the folks at home demand too much of your time. The problem is there is not enough time to get everything done that you are convinced—or others have convinced you—needs to get done.

As a result, someone or something is not going to get what they want from you . . . what they need from you . . . what they deserve from you . . . certainly not what they *expect* from you. There is no way around it. There is just not enough time in your day to be all things to all people. You are going to have to cheat somewhere. Our knee jerk reaction to this dilemma is to answer the call of the squeakiest wheel. Whoever creates the biggest mess ends up with the lion's share of our time and attention. We run from fire to fire, troubleshooting our way through life, rescuing the needy and rewarding those who can't seem to stay out of trouble.

But that certainly isn't strategic and it doesn't solve anything. Over time, our families learn that the only way to get our attention is to create a crisis. And let's face it. It is amazing how much time we can steal from work when our kids are in crisis. Men and women become incredibly bold with their managers, company presidents, and boards when there is a crisis at home. What was unthinkable becomes non-negotiable.

I know a CEO who just spent twenty-nine days with his wife at a detox center six hundred miles from their home. Twenty-nine days. Yet over the past three years he has done almost nothing in terms of investing in what he would tell you now is his most important relationship. And if anyone had suggested he take a twenty-nine-day vacation in order to invest in his marriage, he would have laughed. But he did— only when he had to.

I know a contractor who almost had to shut down his business in order to attend to his daughter's drug addiction. He escorted her from one rehab center to another, trying to find her "the best medical treatment in the country." This is the same guy who could never find the time to complete an entire week of vacation with his family. They left on Saturday; he joined them on Wednesday. But suddenly, he has the time.

Wouldn't you do the same for your wife, your husband, and your kids? Of course you would. So why wait? Why cheat at work when you have no choice? Instead of allowing the most recent crisis to dictate where you cheat, why not allow your cheating to be governed by the greatest purpose? Why not cheat by design?

But how? How does someone cheat at work without destroying her career? And if you cheat your career goals, won't that end up cheating your family in the long run? Can a homemaker cheat her to-do list without cheating her family?

These are complex issues. On paper, there seems to be no solution. But all is not as it appears. For as we will see, when we are willing to reprioritize in a way that honors our Heavenly Father, He is willing to touch down in the midst of our personal chaos and bring the order and balance we so desperately desire.

A MATTER OF PRINCIPLE

Before we go any further, I need to provide you with a word of warning. As I mentioned earlier, this approach to addressing the collision between work and family is held together by a principle.

Principles are powerful things. In the same way gravity affects everything around the earth, a principle influences everything in your personal universe. Whether you are aware of a principle or not, it still applies. You can ignore it, or you can leverage it. But either way, it goes right on affecting your world. You can break a rule, but you can't break a principle. However, if you fail to observe a principle, you can break yourself against it.

The principle in this book will cut right to the heart of your priorities. It will test your loyalty and expose your commitment. When exposed to the light of this simple truth, gray areas will suddenly become either black or white. It will reveal your heart as it relates to your family, your work, and your children. This principle will expose your attitude toward your Heavenly Father as well. It may upset you. It may offend you. But one thing it won't do is lie. If you are ready to take an honest look at yourself, the choices you have been making and why you make them, you are a candidate for change. My prayer is that you can put this principle to work *for* you, before the consequences of ignoring it have a chance to work *against* you.

2

~

A COLLISION COURSE

The collision between work and family is inevitable. And is it any wonder? In our culture work and family make up the two most significant arenas of an individual's life. On average, a person will spend about one-third of his waking life at work. And for many people, a vast majority of the other two-thirds is dedicated to some part of pursuing or maintaining a family. No other aspect of life is more emphasized in our world than work and family.

Even when you're not working or spending time with family, the influence of those two factors follows you wherever you go. Success or failure in either category will have a direct impact on your overall quality of life, your mental outlook, and your self-esteem.

Your sense of identity is determined largely by work and family. Sociologists, psychologists, and philosophers have conducted thousands of studies on the subject. They identify hundreds of different factors, from genetic to environmental. But when you categorize all the data, there are basically two things that shape your sense of identity more than anything else: your work and your family.

That's why one of the first questions asked when two people are getting acquainted is, "So, what do you do?" And not far behind are questions such as, "Are you married? Do you have any children? Do you have any brothers and sisters?"

Knowing *who* you are fulfills a basic human need. Without an answer to that question, a person feels incomplete, inadequate, and insecure. And since work and family play such significant roles in answering it, the pressure is on in both arenas. The natural drive to become established in your career is rivaled only by the desire to have a successful family life. It's only natural that the two become entangled during the rush of daily life.

The irony is that both work and family originate with the same Source: God. He created them to peacefully coexist. The tension between the two is understandable, but it is not unavoidable. Whenever there is destructive tension between two things that are designed to work together, it usually points to "operator error." And when a problem persists, the best thing to do is check with the Manufacturer.

THE ROLE OF WORK

At the climax of creation, God expressed His creativity in an unexpected way:

> The LORD God took the man and put him in the Garden of Eden to work it and take care of it. (Genesis 2:15 NIV)

Before sin, before the fall of man, before the curse, there was work. God made man and placed him in the garden *to work*. From the very beginning, He intended for man to work. Before there was even a family to support, God put Adam to work. It was part of His original plan.

Is that a little surprising? We tend to think of work as being a curse, a consequence of sin. Sure, the nature of work changed a bit after Adam and Eve sinned. God declared that it would be a struggle from then on. He established a relationship between our effort and our provision—a relationship that lures many people to overwork today. Despite those curses, God had the basic concept of work in mind all along. He likes it when we work. He always has. When our attitudes and actions are right, our work is actually very pleasing to God. That's the role of work in its purest form.

Work has been a big part of daily life ever since. Every day, men and women get up at the crack of dawn to plow their vocational fields in order to produce a crop. Presidents lead companies. Salespeople work leads. Homemakers manage households. Some love what they do, and others dream of something better. Whether reluctantly or zealously, we get up each day and work.

THE ROLE OF FAMILY

Whereas work is task-focused, the family is relationship-focused. One is about doing, while the other is about loving. In one environment we find our worth through accomplishment. In the other we find our value simply by who our relatives are. Work is about doing. Family is about being. The members of my congregation want me to show up prepared to speak. My family is happy if I just show up.

By now you are thinking, "Yeah, yeah, I know all of that. I don't need more insight. I need answers. Give me something practical to do."

That is the task-oriented side of you, the "fix it" thing that goes off inside your head whenever there is a problem. And that's not bad. In fact, it is that side of your personality that makes you so effective on the job. But take that God-given drive for progress and accomplishment home with you, and things start to fall apart. You can't "fix" your family. You can't "fix" your marriage. You can't "fix" your kids.

Family requires an entirely different set of tools and standards of evaluation. You do your job. You love your family. It is when we reverse the order that the tension escalates and the tug of war begins.

BALANCING AGENDAS

In God's original plan, there was no conflict between work and family. But when sin entered the world, conflict was introduced into both environments. Man would henceforth struggle at work (Genesis 3:17–19). Women would feel the pain of childbirth (Genesis 3:16). And men and women would struggle in their relationships with one another. (See Genesis 3:16, which implies that Eve would have a desire to rule Adam, but in fact, he would rule over her.) The inherent conflict *within each realm* sets us all up to experience conflict *between* these two realms as well.

Creating a healthy family environment is difficult because of the inherent selfishness of each family member. Creating a successful career is difficult because of the competition in the marketplace. Either one of these environments or the struggles related to both could consume our undivided attention. But we do not have the luxury of devoting our undivided attention to either since most of us find ourselves with the responsibility of both. So we are forced to wrestle with the conflicts of home, work, and the added conflict that arises between the two.

A STRANGE TWIST

With conflict abounding in each of our primary environments, it would seem that our hearts would draw us toward home. After all, in spite of the relational complexities of family, that is where we are most likely to find unconditional acceptance. In contrast to the turnover in the marketplace, at home we are indispensable. At home we have unique roles. It is within the context of family that we are most likely to have our deepest needs met at the deepest level. Besides, isn't work just a way to provide for the family? Clearly one serves the other.

Strange, isn't it—on paper it looks so simple, so cause-and-effect. But in reality work becomes far more than a simple means to an end. For many it becomes *the* end. In spite of the challenges that come with any work environment, there is something about it that is captivating. In spite of the futility, in spite of the insecurity, we are drawn to work. The rewards are tangible, progress is measurable, and the accolades are notable. Before long we aren't working to support our families. We are working to support something far less virtuous—our egos.

Now if you are a stay-at-home mom or dad already scheming about how to slip this book into your spouse's briefcase, stop and think. It could be that you struggle with this as well. Maybe you left the job market years ago and you are still uncomfortable telling people that you don't work outside the home. Why is that? Why isn't there contentment with what you know is the most important job in the world?

Or maybe you struggle with this dynamic in a completely different way. You are fine being a stay-at-home parent. But over time your focus has shifted from the relationship side of staying at home to the task side. You measure your success in terms of neatness, cleanliness, organization, and efficiency. The tasks associated with being a stay-at-home parent are stealing from the joy of being who your partner and children want you to be.

I know of this struggle firsthand as a result of living with the world's most organized woman. Sandra thrives on organization and cleanliness. And I love it. She is incredible when it comes to creating an inviting home environment. But by her own admission, she can become consumed with the environment to the neglect of those who inhabit it.

Just like my marketplace environment, her home environment is full of loose ends. There is always something that needs to be rearranged, organized, cleaned, fixed, replaced, put away, swapped, or returned. Her job is never finished. And to complicate matters, there are four other humans in the house that continually create more for her to do.

The point is work, whether in or out of the house, can become not only an occupation but also a preoccupation. When that happens, the task steals a piece of us that belongs somewhere else. Before long our families begin to sense it. The people who deserve your undivided attention aren't attended to while the projects that could wait are.

I know this is frustrating. You wish I were there so you could tell me to my face, "You don't understand my situation. It is not as simple as you make it sound." And you are right. I don't know the particulars of your situation. But here's what I do know: your Creator does not define your life by your career achievements or the neatness of your pantry. And neither does He define life by the number of hours you spend with your family. There is no lasting contentment in any of those things. A temporary sense of satisfaction and accomplishment, yes. Contentment, no.

Contentment is found neither in the marketplace nor the family alone. It is found when we align our priorities with His as it relates to both areas of responsibility. There is nothing honoring to God about the workaholic who neglects his or her family. But the man or woman who refuses to provide for his family brings no honor to Him either.

Clearly we don't have the luxury of choosing one or the other since both are a permanent part of our lives. Both demand more attention than we have to give. Both originated with our Creator. There's not enough time to get it all done. We are going to say "no" somewhere, either verbally or through neglect. In fact, you are saying "no" now, whether you realize it or not. And that brings us to the question that we must keep coming back to again and again, a question that if answered correctly sets us up to experience the contentment and blessing of God:

Who are you cheating? Better yet . . .

Who feels cheated?

If you work outside the home, chances are it is not your boss or board who feels cheated. You probably don't hear the folks at work complaining that you spend too much time at home.

If you are a stay-at-home mom or dad, it's probably not your children who feel cheated. Your husband or wife probably isn't concerned about how little attention you give the kids. Because of our proclivity to veer in the direction of things that stroke our egos, we tend to cheat at home. We give an inordinate amount of our time, energy, and passion to our work.

PLAYING THE GAME

When confronted with our misappropriation of time and affection, we are all quick to assure our accusers that we do in fact love our families. We talk about what we "wish" we could do, what we have "intended" to do, and what we "plan" to do in the future. We credit ourselves with good intentions. Our guilt is like a salve to our souls. We know we are guilty, but since we know we are guilty, surely there is value in us— surely the fact that we feel bad about what we are doing counts for something! As one young husband blurted out to his wife in his own defense, "But honey, you know my heart!" And he was right, she knew his heart. But it was not his heart that had left her feeling alienated from his life; it was his schedule.

Good intentions have never accomplished anything. If I run over you with my car, but it was my intention to swerve and miss you, you still have to go to the hospital. Upon hearing of my good intentions, your bones are not suddenly healed. You are just as injured as before.

In the physical world that is all too clear. In the world of relationships we live with the illusion that good intentions— the desire of our hearts—somehow heal the wounds we have created with our absence and misprioritization. But all we have to do is think back on our own experience as children to know that nothing could be further from the truth.

If you are a religious person, you may have even taken the "good intention alibi" into the spiritual realm. I have talked to dozens of men and women who have struck a deal with God. This unspoken arrangement goes something like this.

"Lord, You know my heart. You know how badly I want to spend more time with my family. So while I'm away, please watch over and protect them. Please fill the void that I have left while I am away. Lord, I know You understand my love for them; help them to understand it as well."

Granted, you may have never actually prayed a prayer like that one. But if you are expecting God to do your job for you while you do a job for somebody else, essentially that prayer reflects the arrangement you have with God. Now bear with me while I draw a couple of uncomfortable conclusions from that approach to dealing with the fact that there isn't enough time to get everything done. First, we are assuming that God could not just as easily fill the void at work as He could the void at home. Second, we are asking God to fill a gap that only we can fill while we scurry off to do a job that a thousand other people could do. We might as well pray,

"Dear God, You do what only I can do while I go do what many others could do just as well or better."

Kind of convicting, huh?

Does God answer that kind of prayer? I don't know. But in all my years of counseling I can tell you something I have never heard. I have never talked to an adult who reported that while he was growing up his father worked all the time, but God filled in the gaps and there was no residual relational or emotional damage. I have never talked to a mom who reported that her husband neglected his family for the sake of his career, but fortunately God filled the void, and everything was fine.

So where does that leave us? If we can't expect God to cover for us in a way that protects our families from the residual effects of our misprioritization, then what are we to do?

The answer is simple. But it is simple in the way that telling a smoker the solution to his addiction is to stop smoking. It is simple. It is true. But it is not easy to do.

3

~

WATCH FOR
FALLING ROCKS

I met Phyllis Wilson at a leadership conference where she was the keynote speaker. I had never heard her in person, but I had certainly heard of her. In a relatively short time Phyllis had established herself as somewhat of an expert in the field of adolescent behavior and family systems. Her education and her platform ability were a winning combination.

Within the first few minutes of her talk, I knew why Phyllis had become such a sought-after conference speaker. She was one of the most gifted communicators I had ever heard. Frankly, I was somewhat intimidated by her ability to connect so quickly with the audience. Afterward we had an opportunity to chat, and to my surprise she asked if she could come by and talk to me at my office. The tone of her question suggested that she had something specific on her mind. The stage persona quickly drained from her face and was replaced by what I read as panic.

One week later Phyllis showed up in my office looking like she had just come down with the flu. Her face was pale, and it appeared to me that she was having trouble breathing. She barely muttered hello as she slumped down in the chair across the desk from me. "Are you okay?" I asked.

Phyllis wasn't sick, at least not physically. On the night before I heard her speak, she had come home from another speaking engagement and found a note from her husband, Jimmy, on the pillow. The gist of the note was that he wanted Phyllis to leave.

As you might imagine, I began asking questions: Was there another woman? Had there been a big fight? Were there financial issues? Was substance abuse a part of their lives? Was there a problem with the kids?

To these questions Phyllis shook her head. She said, "I'm completely at a loss. He leaves me messages insisting that I pack up and go, but he won't talk to me. He says there is nothing to talk about."

As I read Jimmy's note, there was no bitterness or anger in his tone. He just wanted her out. There was no reason given. It was as if he assumed they both understood what the issue was and that no further discussion was necessary.

Phyllis stared out the window, trying to come up with something to explain Jimmy's behavior. Then she turned back in my direction and shrugged. So I asked her again about the recent past: Was there an event, a defining moment? What did their most recent argument center on?

The last question sparked some interest.

"Argue? That's just it. We never argue," she said.

"About anything?" I asked.

"No," she replied, "in fact we have prided ourselves in the fact that unlike most couples, we don't have arguments."

Now I was starting to understand. So I asked, "If Jimmy were sitting here and I asked him what one thing he would like to change in your marriage, what do you think it would be?"

She managed a smile and said, "Before all of this I would have said he wanted me to be home more. But now I don't know. Now he doesn't want me there at all."

Phyllis finally broke down and began to cry. I say finally, because up until this time she had done a pretty good job retaining her composure. But when she broke, the tears flowed.

Eventually I made contact with Jimmy, and he agreed to come in and talk. But he assured me that he was not going to change his mind and that it would be a waste of my time to try and convince him to do so. I assured him that I was just trying to help Phyllis understand what was going on and that I didn't think it was my responsibility to change anybody's mind.

As it turned out, Phyllis was right. There was no landmark incident that culminated in Jimmy's request. There was no other woman. And she was right about there not being a big argument. Jimmy nodded in agreement when Phyllis reiterated her claim that they never argued.

So what was going on? Why this abrupt shift in affection? Why was Phyllis clueless as to why Jimmy suddenly wanted her out?

THE ARRANGEMENT

Jimmy and Phyllis had an arrangement, not unlike most couples. When Phyllis's career as a conference speaker began to blossom, Jimmy felt like it was his responsibility to be her biggest supporter. As a Website developer, Jimmy had the option of working out of his home and chose to do so in order to give Phyllis the flexibility she needed to travel and leverage her opportunities.

Yeah, Jimmy! What a guy. Probably ought to be nominated as husband of the year. That's what Phyllis thought, and she was quick to give him the credit he deserved. While she was away he held down a full-time job and took care of their two kids.

Now all of that looked good on paper. And everybody's heart was in the right place.

But over time something began to happen in the Wilson household. Nobody could see it, but everybody could feel it. And when they felt it they wrote it off to "That's what we agreed to do."

"Mommy's not here tonight. But she is helping other mommies and daddies know how to be better mommies and daddies for their children."

"I'll be gone again next week, but this engagement has the

potential to open an entirely new set of doors for us. I'll sure miss you."

"We will be fine. We will miss you, but we will be okay. What you are doing is important."

Phyllis was cheating at home. And Jimmy wasn't saying anything about it. Phyllis was taking what belonged at home and selling it to strangers at conferences, and Jimmy was cheering her on. And everybody—with the exception of the kids—was smiling on the outside but dying on the inside. Nobody wanted to admit it, but the arrangement wasn't working, at least not in the way it was being played out.

Jimmy didn't want to nag. After all, this was what he agreed to. Phyllis was starting to believe her own press, and she liked what she was hearing. Add to that, her income was almost double what Jimmy was bringing home. And as much as she loved her family, life on the road was . . . well . . . it was like a continuous party.

Consequently, it was easy for Phyllis to ignore the internal red flags that periodically waved right in front of her face. And when she backed out of the driveway with that perennial cloud of guilt hanging over her, she would remind herself, "This is what we agreed to."

As you might imagine, it was more difficult for Jimmy to maintain a smiling face. Life at home with the kids was not a continuous party. But after a while he became accustomed to Phyllis's absences. In fact, her arrivals began to feel more like interruptions than homecomings. He confided in me, "I got to the point where I would have been just as happy if she had simply mailed us a check and gone on to her next engagement."

Sound extreme? It is. But don't make the mistake of taking comfort in the fact that your situation is not that extreme. For a long time theirs wasn't either. In the beginning their situation was like yours . . . or possibly better. I say that not to scare you, but to wake you up to an insidious dynamic that slowly takes its toll on families who have arrangements like the Wilsons'.

HOLDING ON

Use your imagination for just a moment. Imagine that your best friend walks up to you in your front yard one Saturday and asks you to do him a favor. You have some free time, and so you oblige. He walks over to his car, pops the trunk, and produces a thirty-pound rock.

Now here's where you are really going to have to use your imagination.

At this point he hands you the rock and says, "I really need you to stand here with this rock until I return." He explains why it is important that you stand in that one spot with the rock and that he will return shortly to retrieve it. It is a strange request, and his explanation doesn't make a lot of sense, but this is someone you trust, so you agree. At this point he thanks you profusely and then hops into his car and drives away.

An hour goes by. And what started out as a feasible favor

is beginning to get a little hard. But after all, this is your best friend, so you suck it up and stand there. Another hour goes by and your arms are starting to ache. Everything in you wants to sit down, but you made a promise. Then suddenly, to your relief, your friend pulls in the driveway, jumps out of the car, and runs in your direction. You are so relieved. If you weren't holding the rock, you would hug him.

But your joy is quickly extinguished. Instead of relieving you of your burden he says, "Look, I told you I was coming right back. I was delayed. Here's the deal. I need to run one more quick errand. If you will keep holding the rock, I will make it up to you when I return." Once again, you trust that what you are told is true. If your friend needs to run one more errand before relieving you, that is just the way it is. So you agree. As he turns to go you can't help but blurt out, "Please hurry."

Off your friend goes and there you stand.

Another hour goes by. The sun begins to set. Your muscles are screaming at you to drop the rock. But you refuse to give in. You are committed to holding up your part of the bargain. Besides, your friend said he would make it up to you. You aren't sure what that means, but it must be something good.

Thirty minutes later a car pulls up in the driveway. But someone you don't know is driving. This person walks over and, almost in a whisper, informs you that your friend has been delayed. "Would you mind holding the rock for just a little while longer?" he asks.

The expression on your face is a mixture of pain and anger. You manage to mutter, "Whatever. Just tell him to hurry."

Away the person goes and there you stand. It is dark now. The streets are empty. The neighbors are huddling at their windows watching you stand there, wondering why you would put up with being treated like that by a "friend."

Another hour goes by. You begin to lose your grip. Your arms begin to fall. You tell yourself to hold on, but your body just won't respond. Down goes the rock. And just as it hits the pavement and disintegrates into a hundred pieces, your friend pulls up in the driveway. He jumps out of the car, runs over with a look of panic on his face, and says, "What happened? Did it slip? Did somebody knock it out of your hands? Did you change your mind?" And as he looks for an explanation as to why you *suddenly* dropped the rock, you know that it was a long time coming.

THE EXHAUSTION FACTOR

Now let me explain what happened in terms that will help us later on. Your mental willingness was overcome by your physical exhaustion. You wanted to do what you were asked to do, but after a while you just couldn't do it anymore. Add to that the frustration of being misled about how long you would have to stand there. But even if the aggravation is put aside, at some point you just weren't going to be able to keep holding on. No amount of love, dedication, commitment, or selflessness was going to be able to make up for the fact that your arms were worn out.

Now, just for fun, let's add another element to the story.

You are about to pass out from exhaustion. And finally a car pulls up in the driveway. You are so angry and in so much pain you know you will have to choose your words carefully. Sure enough, it is your buddy. He walks over slowly with one hand behind his back. He forces a smile and says, "I brought you something."

Suddenly, he whips out from behind his back a bouquet of flowers. At that point you don't merely drop the rock, you muster just enough strength to throw it at him! And as he ducks he exclaims, "What was that all about? I brought you flowers, didn't I?"

THE SOUND OF FALLING ROCKS

I probably don't need to apply my little parable. The meaning is pretty obvious. So at the risk of insulting your intelligence, let me be painfully specific:

- When we ask our husbands and wives to carry their load as well as ours, it is like handing them the rock.

- When we are absent at critical junctures in family life, they are left holding the rock.

- When we find ourselves pointing to the future to somehow make up for the past and the present, they are holding the rock.

- When we assure our families that things are going to change and they don't, they are holding the rock.

The interesting thing is, they always accept it. And why not? They love us. They trust us. Besides, we always reassure them that they will only have to hold it for a short time.

Everybody is willing to be "understanding" when a loved one needs to cheat a little. And in real life, cheating is unavoidable from time to time. But when they are left to carry a load they were not created to carry, it is just a matter of time before things will begin to unravel.

There's a point at which that mental willingness succumbs to something our families have no control over. With a literal rock, mental willingness is eventually overcome by physical exhaustion. With the figurative rock, mental willingness is eventually overcome by emotional exhaustion. And when that happens, the rocks come tumbling down.

There's always a final straw: a comment, a phone call, a tired explanation, a no-show, a forgotten birthday, or a missed game. Some little thing that pushes those we love past their ability to hold on. And to the uninformed, unsuspecting spouse—to the husband or wife who has lived with the fantasy that everything is just fine—it seems like a huge over-reaction.

"All I said was . . ."

"All I did was . . ."

But it wasn't the moment. It wasn't the phone call. It wasn't the fact that the big hand was on the six instead of the twelve. It was weeks, months, or possibly years of cheating. The rock finally slipped out of their calloused hands.

You always know when the rock has dropped. There is never any mistaking it. Your straight-A student is failing. Nobody runs to greet you at the door when you finally arrive. Your husband or wife has lost all interest in being intimate.

You hear things such as: "I just can't do this anymore! I can't pretend anymore! I've had enough of your promises! I feel like a single parent!"

When the rock drops, you will do everything in your power to pick it up and piece it back together. As we mentioned in the previous chapter, you will find the time to devote to fixing the problem. But in my experience, when the rock drops, there is always some permanent damage. Most rocks can't be put back together again.

4

⌒

PICKING UP THE PIECES

I'm going to tell you a secret about each of your family members that they will never tell you themselves, primarily because they aren't aware of it. But it is true and extremely important for you to know.

This little secret explains why cheating at home has such a devastating effect on the emotions of our family members. Ironically enough, it also explains why they are so eager to take the rock in the first place.

Do you know what your family wants from you more than anything else?

"Love?" you say.

That's part of it. But it goes deeper than that. They want to feel accepted. In practical terms, they want to feel like they are your priority.

"But they *are* my priority," you might argue.

Granted. They may be your priority, but that's not my point. They want to *feel* like your priority. It is not enough for them to *be* your priority. They must *feel* like it.

I'll never forget discussing this point with a very busy corporate vice president. He kept assuring me of how much he loved his wife and kids. Finally I interrupted him and said, "The problem is, you love your family in your heart, but you don't love them in your schedule. And they can't see your heart."

Every member of your family is an acceptance magnet. Their hearts are drawn toward acceptance. They want to feel your acceptance, your approval, and yes, your love. If you are having trouble connecting the dots, think back to your own childhood. How important was it for you to feel like a priority in your father's world? If you grew up wondering where you fit in his list of priorities, you know the myriad of confusing emotions that filled your childhood and adolescence.

If you grew up with the security of knowing you and the family were clearly *the* priority of his life, you will have a difficult time imagining what it would feel like to grow up without that. But as an adult you can understand the important role his visible love played in your development.

The same is true of your relationship with your mom. Imagine growing up in a home where you had to compete for your mother's attention and affection. Perhaps you don't have to imagine; perhaps you remember. Either way, looking back it is easy for us to understand and appreciate the importance of a family environment where moms, dads, and kids feel like they are the priority.

A measure of loyalty is assumed in every relationship. The

more intimate the relationship, the greater the expectation. Think about your wedding vows . . . Okay, so you can't remember. Well, I wasn't there, but I bet you said something indicating that your spouse was going to be your priority over everything and everybody else. Remember that? It was perfectly appropriate to make that kind of commitment. And now it is perfectly appropriate for your spouse to expect that kind of commitment.

MAKING THE CONNECTION

Now, here's the point: Our family's willingness to hold the rock for us is born out of their desire to please us.

Part of their reason for wanting to please us is that in pleasing us they hope to gain what they value most, our acceptance. They say "yes" with the hopes that their sacrifices will result in a deeper sense of appreciation and love. Their hope is that if they please us, we will find them even more acceptable. Taking the rock—compensating for our busyness, putting up with our absence—is a way to capture and maintain our affection.

There's almost nothing our families wouldn't agree to do if we asked. To refuse our request is to run the risk of disappointing us and possibly losing what is most important. So initially they give us a look that communicates "count on me" and they say, "no problem." But over time the enthusiasm wanes. Over time their looks become ones of intense disappointment. And they are barely able to muster a simple, "We understand."

Now don't check out. This is not psychobabble. This is a

dynamic that is at work right now in the hearts of your spouse and children. This is a dynamic that is at work in your heart as well. Face it. Why do you work so hard? Part of the reason is so that you can *gain approval*. It is not just about the money and the financial security. You want to know that you are okay. And somewhere out there in the marketplace you have found an environment that says you are okay when you perform at a certain standard.

And that is perfectly acceptable. God created you to seek and find approval. That underlying need provides the context for our relationship with Him and everyone else we come into contact with. Again, we are acceptance magnets. We are drawn to environments where our egos are stroked. We flee from environments fraught with rejection.

Here's the problem. When we leave our families holding the rock for too long, their sacrifice becomes a source of the very thing they dread the most—rejection. They go along with us to find approval, and in time the rock that looked like a means to greater acceptance becomes a symbol of rejection. And the longer they hold it, the more rejected they feel.

Whenever you compromise—or cheat—the interests of a family member in order to fill gaps somewhere else, you shuffle your priorities. Loyalty that was intended for a loved one gets displaced and given to someone else. However small, it increases the emotional load they must carry. It may not seem like a big deal. But it sends the message: *You're important . . . but right now something else is more important.* When we take advantage of their willingness to support our dysfunctional schedules and misprioritization, we send a message of rejection.

When you take loyalty that belongs to your family and give it to someone else—your boss, manager, supervisor, coworkers, potential clients, or investors—family members don't feel as if you aren't being as loyal as you should be. They feel rejected.

Again, that's not what you intend to communicate. But actions speak louder than intentions. Nobody can see your heart. Displaced loyalty is translated into rejection, the very thing your family fears most from you.

From your perspective, you're just trying to survive. You have a dozen good reasons to justify shifting your priorities to meet the ever-changing demands at work. But in the economy of human emotions that distinction isn't recognized. If something is more urgent, it must be more important. At least that's how it's perceived and interpreted by your loved ones.

THE CLIENT

Let's get specific. When you can't have dinner with your family because you "can't get out of" having dinner with a client who just flew into town, you send a message to your family: "These clients are more important to me than you." I know that's not how you feel. But how *you* feel is irrelevant. Explaining the importance of the dinner meeting may get them to nod their heads in agreement. But the message is still the same: "Tonight, my priority is somebody else."

Are there times when you are going to be out late? Of course. Are there weeks when you will need to travel? Absolutely. But understand, the message you send is the same. And if you send enough of those messages, they will eventually chip away at the confidence your spouse and kids cling to—confidence that *they* are your priority.

Our instinct is to share our dilemma, seeking empathy and understanding. We think if we can just explain the urgency of the situation, it will somehow change the way everything is interpreted. But in the end, it always feels the same. Cheating at home is translated as rejection. Everything and everyone else are greater priorities, even people we haven't met.

GAUGING OUR SUCCESS

This whole thing would be much easier if everybody in our family had gauges on their foreheads. Gauges are the great thing about cars; you know exactly where you stand. If you run out of gas, it is your own fault. If the engine overheats, you saw it coming.

Wouldn't it be great if our spouse and kids had little acceptance meters? We could come home at the end of the day and check everyone's readings. Then we would know who needs a little extra time and attention. We would know when everybody was charged up enough so it would be safe to ask for a night out with clients. Then we would know when it is appropriate to expect intimacy with our spouses and when we should move in another direction. When everybody was down to a quarter of a charge, we could plan a vacation. Wouldn't that just simplify everything?

Men and women generally respond differently when I suggest the beauty of such a system. The men get all teary-eyed thinking about how much simpler life would be. Women, on the other hand, shake their heads in disagreement. And I know what they are thinking. Women don't want a gauge; they want to be figured out. Taking the time to figure a woman out makes her feel valued.

Now I'm not sure why that is. Women watch men read manuals, pore over articles, and spend countless hours tinkering with stuff, and then we simply ask them, "Hey, what's wrong?"

Now guys, you may hate me for putting this in print for your wife to read, but I don't know any other way to communicate it. You have never walked into your office and asked your computer, "What's wrong?" You've never said to your transmission, "What's wrong?" You have never asked your wide-screen television for a self-diagnosis.

So when you ask your wife to give you a reading, is it any wonder that she says, "Nothing"? Unfortunately for us men, our wives and kids didn't come equipped with gauges. But somewhere between gauges and "nothing," couples must find common ground for the sake of monitoring the vital signs of the family. It's up to each of us to monitor the emotional weight being carried by each of our family members. Through honest, and sometimes awkward, communication we can learn to monitor the hearts of our loved ones.

The gauges on your dashboard are not there to tip you off to the fact that your car is in need of repair. They are there to keep things from getting to that point. When your car breaks down, you don't need a gauge; it is obvious. The advantage of learning to monitor the hearts of our family members is that it enables us to avoid a crisis rather than figure out how to recover from one.

Sandra is the finest woman I've ever met. She is a wonderful wife and mother to our children. There's nothing in the world she wouldn't do for us. I'm convinced she would follow me to the edge of the world if I asked her. She'd even do most of the driving.

Ironically, it is Sandra's intense dedication to the family that makes her hard to read sometimes. Her laid-back manner and endless energy make it easy for me to presume too much. And early on in our marriage, I took unfair advantage of her desire to be super-mom. Like every couple, we had to learn to read the gauges.

My children are the same way. If I judged by appearances alone, I'd have no way of knowing when their gauges were in the red. Like most kids, they each crave Dad's attention. So when I show up, they light up. It would be easy to make incorrect assumptions about what's going in their little hearts.

So in our house we have a very simple system. First, Sandra and I have agreed to avoid saying "nothing" when nothing is untrue. Instead of asking, "What's wrong?" we say something like, "I can tell something is bothering you. When you want to talk about it, I'm available." When I'm having a hard time reading the gauges and need a little help, I say to Sandra, "How are we doing?" That's my way of saying, "I think we are doing allright around here; what do you think?"

With our kids I'm more specific. At least twice a week at bedtime I ask each of them this series of questions:

- Is everything okay in your heart?

- Did anyone hurt your feelings today?

- Are you mad at anyone?

- Did anyone break a promise to you?

- Is there anything I can do for you?

That fourth question is really important to me. I accidentally promise my kids stuff all the time. I say "accidentally" because they hear everything as a promise. "I'll think about it" sounds like a promise to my kids.

FINDING YOUR GROOVE

Now all of that may sound rote. And the last thing you need is another list to remember. But the point is, you've got to slow down long enough to check the family vital signs. We are all better at this than we would like to admit. We generally know when something is up. I say that based on the testimonies of countless couples who all admitted they knew things weren't right. When the rock dropped, they weren't completely surprised. We are rarely blindsided by problems on the home front.

The real issue is whether or not we are willing to pull out of the fast lane long enough to find out what's going on. For someone who has made it a habit to cheat, slowing down to read the vital signs isn't easy. But it is a whole lot easier than getting out of the race completely in order to handle a major crisis.

THE DIVISION TITLE

The reality of this dynamic became even clearer to me the first year our boys played recreation league baseball. On the first and third Wednesdays of each month, I have a meeting that lasts well past 10:00 P.M. On those particular Wednesdays I stay at the office throughout the afternoon and arrive home after the kids are asleep. When our two boys started playing Little League baseball, I sat down with them and explained that I would have to miss some of their Wednesday evening games because of my meeting schedule.

In light of the fact that each of them played two games a week, I would still be able to attend the majority of their games. They understood (there's that word again). In fact, I had Sandra call me in the middle of my meetings when either of our boys got a hit. I could look down at my phone, see her number, and without having to answer know that things were going well on the baseball field.

At the end of that first season, both of my boys' teams had a good chance to win their respective divisions. As I looked at the calendar, however, my oldest son, Andrew, would have his deciding game on a Wednesday evening when I was scheduled to be at the office. Well, there was no way I was going to miss his game, so I told our business administrator I wouldn't be able to attend our meeting. I never mentioned this to Andrew. Actually, I didn't really think he kept up with which Wednesday nights I was out and which ones I was available. But I was mistaken.

The evening before the big game, we were having dinner and I mentioned how much I was looking forward to his game. He immediately looked up at me and said, "But what about your meeting?" I was really surprised. Andrew was only nine at the time, but he was keeping up. I smiled and told him I had canceled my meeting so that I could be at his game. His eyes lit up. He had been under the impression that I wasn't coming. The look on his face told me that I had just made a major deposit with my oldest son. It was one thing for me to be there. It was something else entirely for me to cancel something in order to attend.

They won their game Wednesday night. Two nights later they beat the best team in the league. My son hit a triple and drove in the go-ahead run. His team went on to win the division championship, and he added another trophy to his collection.

Everyone is busy. All of us have more to do than we will ever get done. We all have to cheat along the way. When you cheat strategically, you leverage your busyness for the sake of what's most important. Cheating strategically allows us to communicate the message our families long to *feel*—you are important to me. You are more important to me than anybody or anything else in my world.

5

∽

A DOUBLE-EDGED SWORD

Once again, if you are dying to figure out a way to get your workaholic husband or wife to examine his or her schedule through the lens of these truths, I would suggest you pause long enough to first examine the log in your own eye. My experience is that men and women who cheat at home get way too much support from the people they are cheating.

Remember Phyllis and Jimmy from the previous chapter? When I had a chance to meet with Jimmy, he insisted that their family problems stemmed solely from Phyllis's unwillingness to properly govern her speaking schedule. In his words, "She abandoned the family for life on the road."

After about five minutes of listening to him whine, I held up my hand (terrible counseling technique, I admit) and asked him a question. I said, "Jimmy, did you ever suggest packing up the kids and going with her?"

"Of course not," he said. "The kids are in school, and I have a job to do."

"So," I said, "there's something more important to you than keeping the family together."

He looked puzzled.

I continued. "My point is, you are certain that your family problems stem from Phyllis's unwillingness to prioritize correctly, but aren't you guilty of the same thing?"

He continued to look puzzled.

I pressed on. "What did you do to get Phyllis off the road?"

"Well, we talked about it from time to time," Jimmy said.

"And how did those conversations resolve?" I asked.

"She would agree and promise to cut back," he said, "but nothing changed."

"And what did you do?"

He shrugged and said, "Nothing. What could I do?"

"So you are really a victim, aren't you?" I said.

"Yeah, I guess I am."

Now, I don't do much counseling. The reason being, I am no good at it. It is not that I lack insight. What I lack is patience, tact, etiquette. So at this point in the conversation, I took off my counselor's hat and put on my judge's robe and told Jimmy what a lousy husband and father I thought he was . . . just kidding.

What I did tell him was that if all he had done so far was have a few tame conversations with Phyllis about their situation, he was as much to blame for their crisis as she was.

"What else could I do?" he asked.

"Well, if you had come to me before the most current crisis,"

I said, "and if she refused to reduce her travel, I would have suggested you pack up and go with her."

"That would have wreaked havoc with our kids and our finances," he said.

Finally, I regained my counseling composure and paused. I waited a long time until what he had just said began to sink in.

He smirked. "I get it."

He leaned back, stared out the window, and said, "The kids are a wreck as it is, and I can't concentrate at work. I don't know if it would have gotten her off the road, but I doubt it would have made matters any worse."

LOVE AND LEARN

Jimmy and I went on to talk about all the ways he contributed to the problem. By the time we were finished, he admitted that he had major reservations about her road trips to begin with. He wanted to support his wife's budding career. No one can blame him for that. But looking back, the timing was terrible and he knew it but was afraid to put his foot down.

Afraid of what? Afraid of the thing we all fear in family relationships, rejection. As is so often the case Jimmy took the rock to avoid rejection and, as a result, felt the full force of it. He thought he was being a loving, understanding spouse when in reality he was simply facilitating his own failure as a husband and father. And one day he just couldn't handle it anymore, and the rock dropped. His emotional exhaustion overwhelmed his willingness to be a supportive husband. What he wanted so badly to avoid became a raging reality. And to compound his confusion, now he looked like the bad guy for leaving.

Husbands and wives are hesitant to put their foot down because they feel like they are betraying their commitment as a supportive spouse. Nothing could be further from the truth. Unfortunately, men and women wait so long that by the time they finally do something, they are so exhausted they feel like their only option is to bail out completely.

To facilitate your husband or wife's misprioritization is to add to your own dysfunction. Sure it's uncomfortable. But it is only going to get more uncomfortable with time. I know it feels like you are being unsupportive. But the truth is, you are supporting what needs supporting most. All of us need a reality check every once in a while. Nobody stays in the middle of the road without lines and guard rails. On more than one occasion Sandra has looked at me and said, "I'm beginning to feel like a single parent."

MUTUAL SUBMISSION

If you are a Christian, you may find yourself wrestling with issues of submission and unconditional love and a myriad of other biblical concepts that support your paradigm for marriage. Maybe you do remember your marriage vows. Perhaps your takeaway from everything the pastor had you repeat that Saturday afternoon was, "Grin and bear it." How else could you interpret, "'Til death us do part"?

But before you hunker down for another season of neglect, you need to know that you are not getting any brownie points in heaven. Submission has nothing to do with fulfilling a role you were not designed to fill. That's not submission. That's emotional suicide. God isn't going to honor that.

Facilitating your husband or wife's irresponsible behavior and unhealthy priorities is not an act of love. You wouldn't consider it an act of love for someone to sell your underage son or daughter a pack of cigarettes, would you? Why not? Well, because it is not good for them.

Exactly.

Now I'm sure I will have to fight with my publisher to keep this next sentence in my manuscript. But I surely believe it with all my heart. If your marriage is headed toward a crisis anyway, go ahead and have it while you still have your wits about you. Call the question. Show up at work. Pack up the kids. Hide the keys. Do something. But for your sake and the sake of your marriage, don't wait until you are so beaten down that there seems to be only one option.

THE SUPREME EXAMPLE

As a Christian I believe we find in Christ an example of unconditional love and a call to uncompromising accountability. He laid down his life for us. But he told us how to live in no uncertain terms. He saw no contradiction between the two because there is none.

Christ honored us by considering our needs before His own. At the same time He honored us by laying down the laws of relationship and holding us accountable to them. He promised to never leave or forsake us in one breath and yet warned us of the practical consequences of refusing to honor the Son in the next. He accepted us the way we were but loved us too much to leave us in our original state. He submitted Himself while at the same time requiring our submission. It is through mutual submission that the created and the Creator experience intimacy. And so it is with a husband and wife.

WORK IT OUT

So what does that look like in your marriage? Unfortunately I can't tell you that. But suffering in silence is not an option. Complaining to your friends isn't a solution either.

Whatever you do, don't sit idly by while your self-esteem slowly erodes away. Don't allow the current dysfunction to continue chipping away at your ability to cope with the normal stresses of everyday life. Do something now while you are still strong enough to weather the ensuing storm. Do something now before you feel like your only option is to run.

Regardless of how strong or committed you are, eventually you'll exceed your emotional limits. Sooner or later, mental willingness will be overcome by emotional exhaustion. When you reach that point, you will do something. But odds are it will be something you regret.

That's precisely what happened to Jimmy. Rather than confront Phyllis, he waited. In fact, he waited and prayed. He prayed that God would change Phyllis's heart and bring her home. But God didn't answer his prayer. And so when he couldn't handle it anymore, he did the very thing he criticized her for. He left.

As bad as things were, Jimmy regrets leaving. He regrets it primarily for his children's sake. It is a memory he hopes time will erase. And maybe it will. But in the meantime Jimmy can't forget the panicked look on his kids' faces as he gathered their belongings, hurriedly packed their suitcases, and rushed out the door before Phyllis arrived. For him, those two days are a nightmare he relives again and again. He sees insecurity in the eyes of his children he has never seen before.

Was he wrong to leave? I don't know. But I'm glad something happened. For the first time they are talking about a situation that should have been addressed years ago. Phyllis doesn't want to give up her traveling completely, but she sees the value in cutting back. I think she is afraid to come home. She still feels like a stranger.

Although it took a while, Jimmy is able to see how his good intentions contributed to their issues. He is still angry. But he realizes that part of his anger is self-directed. He is learning to say "no" to Phyllis. And strangely enough, I think she actually likes it.

HOME SECURITY

In the next section we are going to address in very specific terms what to do when there is too much to do. But before we shift gears, I want to draw your attention one last time to the relationship between cheating at home and the emotional strain that creates. Every time you cheat your family—no matter how trivial—it represents a draw against someone's emotional strength. Every time.

Regardless of how much money you have in the bank, when you make a withdrawal, you have a little less. Regardless of how happy and healthy your family is, when you take what is expected at home and give it to someone or something else, you have made a withdrawal. If the deposits don't vastly outnumber the withdrawals, there will be tension. The tension will ruin the joy of coming home. When you no longer enjoy coming home, you will look for more reasons to stay away. That, of course, only makes things worse.

If there were physical rocks or visible gauges, our job would be easier. It would be next to impossible for us to lose sight of this important relationship. But there are no rocks. And the family doesn't come equipped with gauges. Yet the relationship is there. It is real. The emotional and relational well-being of our family is at stake. The moral well-being of our children is at stake. And we have the change in our pockets to ensure that the necessary deposits are made on time.

This is difficult work. But it is your only unique responsibility. On the marketplace side of the equation, you are expendable. Even if you own your own company, you are expendable. You know that. At home, you play a unique role. You are the only father or mother your children will ever have.

The health of your marriage determines the environment in which your kids grow up.

Even if the tension in your family never reaches crisis proportion, why allow any unnecessary tension? Why not address the undercurrents? Your home environment defines what your children perceive as "normal." Create for them what you hope they will recreate when it is their turn.

I know what you're thinking: "But what about my job? What about my career? So far you have done nothing to help me know how to balance all of that."

We'll get to those concerns next. But as we will see in the beginning of the next section, *what* precedes *how*. Until you have made up your mind to quit cheating at home, it is pointless to talk about how everything is going to pan out. You have to make up your mind before you determine the feasibility of your decision.

Sound backwards? This isn't the first time you have approached a decision this way.

Remember when you decided to get married? Did you have all the *how to*'s worked out? Probably not. You decided marriage was the thing to do and you went for it. And once the decision was made, you came up with a workable plan. It entailed some sacrifice and some creative financing. But you made it work. Why? Because love conquers all!

You are going to need the same passion and blind determination with this decision as you did with that one. And when you do, you will have made more than a domestic decision. You will have made a spiritual one as well. For in choosing to put your family first, you have brought your priorities in line with those of your heavenly Father. And when a man or woman surrenders his or her will to the Father, He takes responsibility for the outcome of the journey.

SECTION II

~

Cheating by the Book

We should not be surprised to find this principle illustrated in the Scripture. In fact, this principle is found throughout Scripture. Chances are, your favorite Bible story involves someone giving to God what somebody else believed belonged to them. And the reason you love the story is because God came through on behalf of the individual who cheated man rather than God. Daniel was one such man. Actually, at the time of this story, Daniel was only a teenager . . .

6

~

A TALE OF TWO KINGS

About 605 B.C. the Babylonians invaded Jerusalem. Rather than destroy the nation itself, the Babylonians sought instead to destroy the Israelites' identity and culture. They made Israel a slave state. As part of the process they handpicked the best and the brightest of the youth and shipped them off to be immersed in Babylonian culture and turned into model Babylonians. Daniel was among the potential converts. He was taught a new language, and given a new wardrobe and a new name.

Apparently, Daniel was okay with these changes. But then his new masters demanded something of Daniel that he couldn't go along with.

Then the king ordered Ashpenaz, chief of his court officials, to bring in some of the Israelites from the royal family and the nobility—young men without any physical defect, handsome, showing aptitude for every kind of learning, well informed, quick to understand, and qualified to serve in the king's palace. He was to teach them the language and literature of the Babylonians. The king assigned them a daily amount of food and wine from the king's table. (Daniel 1:3–5a NIV)

Daniel drew the line when it came to his diet. Eating from the king's table had overtones that Daniel was not comfortable with. It wasn't so much the food as much as it was what the food symbolized. Traditionally, the Babylonians worshiped their pagan gods through offerings of meat and wine. After they offered the meat and wine to the gods, the leftovers were eaten by the king and his court as a final gesture of loyalty. Eating the food offered to the Babylonian gods was a symbol of submission to their authority. By eating the food, participants acknowledged the gods as the source of their provision and strength. In Daniel's case, it would in effect be giving the Babylonian gods credit for his wisdom and abilities. And that constituted a clear violation of Daniel's loyalty to the God of Israel.

Humanly speaking, Daniel had every reason to go along with the demands of his captors. Why remain loyal to a God who had so clearly abandoned him? Daniel had been forcefully taken from his home. His family was probably missing or dead. He had been stripped of his identity. His nation and culture had been destroyed. Why remain loyal to a God who would allow all of that? Besides, this was his big break.

Instead of killing him, they were grooming him to be a model citizen. Instead of being assigned to some meaningless work detail, he was being trained to serve in the king's palace. Instead of starving, he was offered the same food the king eats. Why rock the boat? Besides, what was God going to do? What more could He do? Everything of any value had already been taken away.

Daniel had no reason to fear God. The damage was done. It was time for Daniel to fend for himself. Or at least, it would seem so.

Daniel's situation is not unlike ours. There were two parties who wanted something from Daniel, and he could not satisfy the demands of both. He would either give the visible king, King Nebuchadnezzar, what he expected or give the invisible King, the Lord God, what He deserved. There was no way to satisfy both. He could either violate his conscience and hope God would understand or violate the king's expectations and hope the Babylonians would understand.

Now think about it. Which would you have chosen? In one corner, you have your God . . . patient, loving, merciful. Certainly He would cut you some slack in a situation like that. In the other corner you have the Babylonians . . . ego-centric, merciless, violent, those who slaughtered your family and destroyed your hometown. What are the odds they are going to change the rules because of your religious preference? They are committed to erasing this preference from the face of the earth.

Either way, Daniel had to choose. He had to commit himself to one side or the other. Either he would cheat God of the devotion He deserved or cheat the Babylonians of the cooperation they demanded.

Isn't it interesting that when we look at Daniel's situation, the "right" thing to do is clear to us? And because we know how the story turned out, we applaud his courage. In fact, this is the kind of story we want our children to read and to learn from. We would consider ourselves successful parents if our teenagers had that kind of courage in the face of temptation. If you are a Christian, chances are this is a story you have read to your children. In your own way you have said to your kids, "Be like Daniel. Do the right thing even when it costs you something."

But when we look at our circumstances, we lose sight. Somehow our situation is different. In fact, you may be arguing with me even now.

"It's not that simple."

"You're not making a fair comparison."

"My circumstances are different."

"That was then, this is now."

"I'm not Daniel!"

Maybe you're right. Maybe your circumstances are too difficult for God. Maybe you should get a special permission slip. After all, Daniel's life was on the line. And what's at stake for you is far more critical than that. If you were to side with your family and let the chips fall where they may at the office, they might . . . well, you could lose . . . who knows what the consequences might be? And that is the point. Who knows what would happen? You think you do. But you are only guessing. And besides, God may want to do something unusual. But now I'm getting ahead of myself.

A QUESTION OF LOYALTY

Daniel's choice of diet was an indication of where he placed his loyalty. For us, the chief indicator is time. Daniel's loyalty was tested by what he ate. Ours is tested by what we put on our calendars. Where you spend your time is an indication of where your loyalties lie. In effect, you pledge your allegiance to the person or thing that receives your time.

We don't generally associate time with loyalty when it comes to self-evaluation. We make the connection when we evaluate other people, but not ourselves. If someone refuses to give you time, you make a judgment about his or her commitment to you. But we evaluate our own sense of loyalty differently. We judge our loyalties by how we *feel*.

If I were to ask you how loyal you were to your family, you would answer in extreme terms. If I ask for evidence of your loyalty, chances are your answer would not center on the amount of time you spend with them. You would talk about how you felt, what you have done, how far you would go to protect them, provide for them, and so forth. All of this is evidence of how you feel toward your family.

But the chief indicator from your family's perspective is

different. It boils down to time. The problem is, your employer and client judge your loyalty to them in the same terms. Time. And there is not enough time to go around. So, similar to the story of Daniel, there is a choice to make. He couldn't eat without eating the king's required rations. And if you are like most people, you cannot give all the time expected/required of you to both work and family. Somebody is going to get cheated.

FAITHFUL WHEN FAITHLESS

As you may remember, Daniel decided to disappoint the visible king and cast his fate with the Invisible King, the One who had not done much for him lately. He decided to remain faithful in spite of God's seeming unfaithfulness.

But Daniel resolved not to defile himself with the royal food and wine . . .

This is how lasting change begins. It begins with a decision. Before Daniel knew the outcome of his decision, before he understood how he would address the issue with his supervisors, he made up his mind. He decided, regardless of the outcome, "I will not abandon my allegiance to my Invisible King."

Don't rush by this. Whenever I talk to men and women about redirecting their cheating, they always respond the same way. "But if I do that . . . " And then they proceed to tell me the future. Suddenly they become fortunetellers. They tell me what will happen at work, what will happen to their bonuses, what will happen to their reputations. It is amazing the clarity they have about future events. I am being facetious, of course. But they speak with such authority I am always tempted to ask for stock advice while they are peering into their crystal balls.

Once they finish telling me what they are sure will happen, they tackle the next tier, the "what abouts":

What about the kids' college?"

"What about our financial goals?"

"What about the mortgage?"

That's when I pull out my crystal ball and say, "If something doesn't change, you aren't going to need to worry about retirement because you aren't going to retire together anyway. Furthermore, your kids' college fund is going to be used up paying attorneys' fees. And instead of worrying about how to pay the mortgage, you need to decide which one of you will assume it when you aren't living together anymore."

You see, this principle cuts both ways. There is a price to pay either way you go. But for some reason we only look into the future through one set of lenses. And then when our mis-prioritizing comes home to roost, we wonder what happened.

LOOKING AHEAD

I'm sure Daniel had an inkling of what would happen if he sided against the visible king. But he didn't let that stop him. And once his mind was made up, he came up with a plan. A terrible plan. An unreasonable plan. Get this: he decided to ask his captors if they would change the rules for him!

[A]nd he asked the chief official for permission not to defile himself this way. (Daniel 1:8 NIV)

Can you imagine?

There's a familiar scene from the musical *Oliver* that captures the absurdity of Daniel's presumption. If you have seen the movie, you will no doubt remember it. Oliver, the little orphan boy, sheepishly approaches the cruel master of the orphanage with his empty bowl and utters, "Please sir, I want more." The dining hall is silent as every other orphan watches in amazement. Nobody asks for more. What was he thinking? And sure enough, the orphanage master lets loose his rage on the poor orphan child who didn't know any better than to ask for seconds.

Why would Daniel make such a ridiculous request? Probably because he didn't have any choice. He had made up his mind. He might as well see if anybody would go along with him. But what were the chances that his captors would bend the rules for him? Humanly speaking, none. Zero. But that's where the story takes an interesting twist, one that Daniel had not necessarily counted on but one he knew was a distinct possibility.

Now God had caused the official to show favor and sympathy to Daniel. (Daniel 1:9a)

The "now God" factor changed everything. What on the surface looked like an impossibility became a reality. Not because of Daniel's wit and insight, but because God decided to honor Daniel for where he placed his loyalty. God's "now" and our "now" are never in sync. I'm sure Daniel would have preferred that God not wait until the last minute to intervene. Things would have been much less stressful if the official had come to him first and suggested a different diet. But that is usually not God's way.

Apart from "now God," it was clear to all those looking on what Daniel's fate would be. As you evaluate the notion of reprioritizing your time, you are probably faced with some dark realities as well. This is why most of us, once we are to the edge of the precipice, turn around and retreat to what we know.

I tried my hand at surfing once. Everything went well until the moment when I had to stand up on the board. Peering down over the edge of the wave sapped my courage. I felt like I was looking down from the top of a building. Time after time I tried to muster the courage to stand, and every time I retreated from the challenge. It looked so easy from the shore. But I just couldn't commit. The unknown was terrifying.

So it is with those of us who have grown comfortable with the life we have created for ourselves in the marketplace. Though we consider ourselves risk takers, the fact is, we cower at the prospect of saying "no" to lucrative opportunities. We are scared to death to leave early. The idea of losing a sale over an extra couple of hours at home causes us to cringe. So we paddle our way to the edge of the wave, take one look, and retreat to what we know, to what we can control.

There would have been no "now God" moment for Daniel had he not made up his mind and charged ahead. There will be no "now God" moment for you, either, until you place your loyalty where it belongs and give Him an opportunity to intervene on your behalf. And the tragedy is, you will spend your entire life and never know what God would have done in response to your faith in Him.

THIS IS A TEST

In spite of the official's fondness for Daniel, there were factors that limited what he could do on his Jewish friend's behalf.

> Now God had caused the official to show favor and sympathy to Daniel, but the official told Daniel, "I am afraid of my lord the king, who has assigned your food and drink. Why should he see you looking worse than the other young men of your age? The king would then have my head because of you." (Daniel 1:9–10 NIV)

When Daniel realized that his request put the king's official in danger, he suggested a compromise, a test of sorts:

> Daniel then said to the guard whom the chief official had appointed over Daniel, Hananiah, Mishael and Azariah, "Please test your servants for ten days: Give us nothing but vegetables to eat and water to drink. Then compare our

appearance with that of the young men who eat the royal food, and treat your servants in accordance with what you see." So he agreed to this and tested them for ten days. (Daniel 1:11–14 NIV)

Daniel was not insensitive to the predicament his unusual standards created for his new friend. So he approached the situation diplomatically. He gave the official an out. But he didn't agree to compromise his convictions if the outcome of the test didn't suit the official. If you attended Sunday school as a child, you probably remember what happened next:

At the end of the ten days they looked healthier and better nourished than any of the young men who ate the royal food. So the guard took away their choice food and the wine they were to drink and gave them vegetables instead. To these four young men God gave knowledge and understanding of all kinds of literature and learning. And Daniel could understand visions and dreams of all kinds.

At the end of the time set by the king to bring them in, the chief official presented them to Nebuchadnezzar. The king talked with them, and he found none equal to Daniel, Hananiah, Mishael and Azariah; so they entered the king's service. In every matter of wisdom and understanding about which the king questioned them, he found them ten times better than all the magicians and enchanters in his whole kingdom. (Daniel 1:15–20 NIV)

Basically, Daniel and his friends got a promotion and a raise.

If you are ready to redirect your cheating, three things are probably going to be required. I say "probably" because I think this narrative is an illustration, not a blueprint. First, you've got to make up your mind. You've got to decide to quit cheating at home before you know how you are going to pull it off, before you know how things are going to sort themselves out.

Once you have made up your mind, you need to come up with a plan—an exit strategy from your current schedule—and present it to your employer. And, like Daniel, your request may appear absolutely ridiculous. But that is only because you don't know what God may want to do on your behalf. Then, like Daniel, you need to set up a trial.

In the remaining chapters we will look at each of these steps in detail.

7

⁓

MAKE UP YOUR MIND

Choosing not to cheat at home begins with a decision. A decision to quit cheating.

You can't wait until you know how the story is going to end. You can't wait until all the details have been worked out. You can't wait until another job comes along that doesn't demand such an arduous travel schedule. The decision to stop cheating must precede all of that.

Daniel didn't discover a weak spot in the Babylonian chain of command and exploit it. He made up his mind. Daniel didn't know *how*. He didn't know the *where* or *when*. But he knew the *what*. He made up his mind from the beginning that he would not defile himself, regardless of the outcome.

That's important. As the verses that follow explain, there would be other things Daniel did, too. There would be negotiations with the Babylonian authorities, details would be discussed, and the gaps would be filled in along the way. But all of that came later. In the beginning, there was only Daniel and his decision to take from Nebuchadnezzar and give to God.

JUST IMAGINE

I realize I have already made this point in at least four other chapters. But this is the sticking point. Once you get by this, the rest is . . . well, it's all hard. But either way, you can't start exploring future possibilities until you have made up your mind.

The temptation is to substitute a commitment with a condition.

"When I . . ."

"If they . . ."

I've never seen that work. You may be the exception. If so, write me and tell me about it. Before you commit to a conditional decision (if that even makes sense), gather your family together and explain it to them. Look 'em directly in the eyes and say, "You are so important to me that if such and such happens, I am going to give you more of my undivided time and attention." Then clarify it for them. Say, "You see, such and such is *more important* than you are. So unless such and such happens, I will have to remain on my present course."

You get the point. Once you make your commitment conditional, you have just underscored the fact that your spouse and the kids really aren't the priority after all. How would you feel if your daughter came home and said she was committed to staying a virgin as long as she got asked to the prom? What kind of commitment is that? What if your son told you he was committed to never cheat on an exam as long as he knew all the answers? Okay, maybe it is an unfair comparison. But in terms of emotional impact, I'm not as far off as you might think.

Now imagine this scenario. Imagine sitting down with your family, looking them in the eye, and saying, "Mommy hasn't been home as much as she should. I'm committed to changing that. I'm not sure how just yet. But things are going to change. And they are going to change quickly. You are more important to me than anything or anybody else in the world."

Powerful, huh? And I bet that's genuinely the way you feel. So let's put some feet on it. Commit.

That was the first step for Daniel, and it's the first step for you and me. It all begins with a decision—before you know how the details are going to work out. You may not know how your boss is going to react. You can't predict what will happen financially or with your position at work. But in spite of the uncertainty, you can make up your mind not to cheat your spouse or your family any longer, no matter what. End of conversation.

PREFERENCE VERSUS CONVICTION

Now, I know I'm a preacher. And it is easy for men and women in the business community to excuse themselves from a discussion facilitated by someone who clearly doesn't understand the complexities of their work environment. But for future reference, when is the last time you heard about someone in business going into the ministry because the business environment was too stressful? I'm not looking for sympathy. I just don't want to give you any wiggle room in light of what I'm about to say.

Reprioritizing your world around your family is not just a good idea. It is a God idea. As a Christian, I don't think I have any option when it comes to establishing my priorities. To ask my family to take the leftovers is more than insensitive. It flies in the face of everything we are taught in the New Testament about the family.

Nowhere in Scripture are you commanded to lay down your life for your stock options. Or to love your career like Christ loved the church. We are instructed to *do* our jobs and *love* our families (see Colossians 3:23). When you *love* your job and *do* your family, you've not only stepped outside the bounds of family life, you have stepped outside the will of God.

You can't take the scriptural admonitions concerning marriage seriously without prioritizing your relationships at home over work. It is impossible. As my dad is fond of saying, "God doesn't reveal His will for our consideration. He reveals it for our participation." From God's point of view, this is not a helpful option. This is an imperative. It is part of God's plan for you as a parent and spouse. Obedience in this area opens you up to the blessings and faithfulness of God at home and at work.

As the story of Daniel reiterates, there's something about

an all-or-nothing conviction that activates the divinely driven forces of the universe on your behalf. Following the principles of God results in the blessings of God.

THE AFTERMATH

On the human side of the equation, there are two big benefits to making up your mind in the face of uncertainty.

#1: Momentum

Conviction is essential because only something as powerful as a heartfelt conviction could reverse the misdirected momentum caused by your misprioritization. The wheels are turning. The ball is rolling. The problem is everything is moving in the wrong direction. You have momentum, but it is taking you farther and farther away from your goal. How do you stop that? How do you turn it around?

You make up your mind.

Conviction is like a bat in the hands of Barry Bonds. A 90-miles-per-hour fastball moving in the direction of the catcher is suddenly transformed into a 120-miles-per-hour rocket headed into center field.

You need something to reverse your momentum. A conviction has the power to do just that.

Let's face it. Our world is resistant to change. Old habits die hard. Chances are, there will be significant changes necessary to neutralize the friction between work and family in your life. It's amazing how change-resistant your world can become the minute you set out to break the molds. So you'll need all the momentum you can get.

There will be obstacles to overcome and problems to solve. From where you sit now, you can't fully anticipate the challenges or their solutions. But you can resolve to maintain an unwavering stance when it comes to your priorities. And when the dark clouds of uncertainty come and there are no answers for the moment, your momentum might turn out to be the one thing that carries you through to the other side.

It's a simple matter of physics. When you're going up against an obstacle bigger than you are, momentum is the only equalizer. What you can't muster in terms of mass, you can make up for in velocity. And that could be the deciding factor between success at work and home, or compromise in both places.

#2: Focus
A firmly held conviction sharpens your focus.

When you commit to a direction, it narrows your options. And that in turn forces you to focus only on the options that will lead to the desired results. The reason Daniel proposed an alternative diet is because it was his only option, given his conviction. When you eliminate certain options, it's amazing how resourceful you become. Conviction eliminates options.

When Hernando Cortez landed at Veracruz, Mexico, on April 21, 1519, he ordered the ships in his fleet to be burned. His reason? His goal—his *conviction*—was to conquer Mexico for Spain. He knew he and his men would face many obstacles. They would be forced to confront Aztec, Cuban, and Mayan warriors. As long as there were ships to retreat to, retreat would remain an option. But retreat was not an option for Cortez. His conviction, and his decision to burn the ships, eliminated at least one option. That symbolic gesture rallied his troops to focus all their resources on achieving victory. In an amazingly short amount of time, Mexico was theirs.

Making up your mind not to cheat your family anymore is a decision. Interestingly, the Latin root for the word, *decidere*, means, "to cut off." Deciding not to cheat at home involves "cutting off" those behaviors and habits that are contrary to your new conviction. Making up your mind is not just about choosing an option. That's only half the story. It's also about thoroughly eliminating all competing options. Choosing results in focus.

Eliminating options is part of what makes this process so painful. Giving up good things for the sake of what's best is not easy, even when we are convinced it is right.

I know for many the prospect of giving up even a portion of the accolades, financial rewards, and emotional strokes associated with the marketplace is extremely difficult. We are always tempted to look for a way around the necessity of missing out on tangible rewards. The lure of recognition keeps many from ever acting on their "conviction" to go home. But you can't have it both ways. Just as you have missed out on some of the rewards of being what God has called you to be at home, now you must embrace the prospects of missing out in the marketplace.

What are you afraid of losing as a result of redirecting your cheating? What do you know you will have a tendency to try and hold onto in spite of your decision to reprioritize? It is important for you to know exactly what that is. Because chances are, that thing, that relationship, that perk, perhaps that hobby, may eventually become the thing God uses to seal your commitment one way or the other. That may be the ship you have to burn. And in burning it, you may send the clearest message you have ever sent to your family about their priority in your life.

THE GIFT

On many occasions I have talked with men who confided that it was not their work that was the point of contention in their home. It was a hobby. For some, it was the time they spent at the gym. For others, their mistress was the golf course. For one very close friend, it was his bicycle.

In his early twenties, Mike was an Olympic hopeful. He came very close to making the 1988 Olympic team. When I met Mike, he was 37 and continued to compete and to win. Riding through the mountains of North Georgia was more than an afternoon event. For Mike, it was a passion. It was not uncommon for Mike to ride one hundred miles in a weekend.

But riding was not a family event. It was time reserved for Mike and his buddies. And it was time that could have, and as

Mike later admitted, should have, been given to his wife, Angela, and their eight-year-old daughter.

Like most wives, Angela believed Mike loved her more than his bicycle. But she didn't feel it. She *knew* his heart but she *felt* his schedule. Mike did everything imaginable to play both sides of the aisle. He offered to take Angela with him on biking weekends. He entered fewer races. But as long as his bicycle hung in the garage, it served as a point of contention. Even when Mike was home on Saturdays, she knew he would rather be out riding. Angela felt like she was competing with rubber and aluminum.

I'll never forget the Sunday afternoon Mike showed up at my house with his mountain bike. "Here," he said. "I want you to have this."

I assumed he wanted me to hold onto it for a while, which I was more than happy to do.

"No," he said. "I'm giving it to you. No more biking."

I was shocked. To begin with, this was a $2000 bike. But more than that, I knew Mike's love for biking.

"This is something God has wanted me to do for some time. I thought there was a way around it. But there wasn't," Mike said. "So, here it is. Have fun."

I asked how Angela responded. I was sure she was as surprised as I was. But I had a feeling she felt more than simple surprise. Mike confirmed my suspicion.

"Her heart melted," he said. "She cried when I told her. She told me I didn't need to get rid of it for good. But I insisted. I think she feels more loved by me now than ever before."

Later, Angela said, "I never thought Mike would give it up. Nothing he has ever done has meant more to the kids and me. I know how much he loved to ride. For him to walk away from his bikes is . . . well . . . I feel like we are his priority again."

For Mike, there was a bridge to burn. Giving away his bike removed an option. Now it would be easier for him to focus.

What about you? Are there bridges you need to burn? What are the bridges that making this decision will require you to burn? Are there accounts you need to hand off? Are there some out-of-town meetings that need to be handled on the phone? Is there an offer you need to refuse? A promotion you need to give back? Once you have made up your mind, it will become all too clear what stands in the way of your being able to focus on your commitment to reprioritize.

A STAKE IN THE GROUND

Making up your mind will require some specific commitments. They may appear to be impractical at first. That's okay. We will discuss how to get from here to there in the next chapter. For now, let's be impractical. What exactly are you committing to do? Spending *more* time at home and *less* time at the office isn't specific enough.

The more specific you are about the results you feel called

to achieve, the easier it will be to follow through. And the easier it will be for others to hold you accountable.

Daniel was pretty specific: no meat and wine from the king's table. That was his non-negotiable.

So what is your non-negotiable? What does it look like? Does it mean leaving the office everyday at 5:30, regardless? Does it mean never missing one of your children's performances or ball games? What does this commitment look like in your world?

Again, promising to do "better" won't get it. You've already done that. That terminology doesn't even register with your family. They've heard that before.

I know this is scary. It is easier to be vague. When you are vague you have the advantage of feeling like you are making progress, but with none of the liabilities of a specific promise. We've all played that game. Everybody feels better for the moment, but nothing changes.

Let's start with this question: What change would your spouse most like you to make in regard to your schedule?

I'll never forget the afternoon I asked Sandra that question. She didn't hesitate. She looked right at me and said, "I would love for you to be home by 4:00 every afternoon."

At the time we had two preschoolers and a third child on the way. By 4:30 she was done. She had given all she had to give. When I came stumbling through the door at 5:30 or 6:00, she was running on fumes. In that same conversation she informed me that 4:00 to 6:00 were the two most difficult hours of the day. If she could change anything about my schedule, she would have me home during those two hours.

Now let me put that conversation in the broader context of my professional life so that you can understand my predicament.

TAKING CARE OF BUSINESS

My little chat with Sandra took place one month after I had agreed to help pioneer what eventually became North Point Community Church. If you've ever started anything—whether it's a new church or a new business—you know that start-ups of any kind require limitless time, attention, and energy. Our staff was lean, we had few members, money was very tight, and every resource was stretched thin.

Meanwhile the demands were starting to pile up. And at that point in the life cycle of an organization, you need 100 percent from everybody—especially the leader.

Leaving the office in time to be home by 4:00 seemed like a terrible idea. At least from the standpoint of leading a start-up organization. One thing working in my favor was the fact that our offices were literally ten minutes away from our home. But that still meant leaving a few minutes before 4:00.

As we continued to talk, she agreed that if I left the office at 4:00, it would still make a big difference. As Sandra and I evaluated our whole situation, discussed our schedules, and took an honest look at where we were as a family, it became apparent that if I was committed to making her and the kids feel like my priority, I would have to limit my time at work to forty-five hours a week.

That seemed very extreme at the time. I didn't know of any pastor who only worked 45 hours a week. I didn't know any professional of any kind who had a forty-five-hour workweek. I felt guilty. I felt like I wasn't being a good example to the rest of the staff. And frankly, I wasn't convinced that I could build a church with that kind of schedule.

But that was the commitment I made. Leaving at 4:00 and working a forty-five-hour workweek were my non-negotiables. I'm not recommending that for anyone else. That's just where we were, and that's what I felt like I needed to do.

So in my own way, I made a deal with God. Essentially I said, "Lord, feel free to build whatever kind of church You can build with forty-five hours of my time. You know that's all I have right now."

As a result of my decision, there were meetings that got cut short because I was committed to leaving at a certain time. There were programs I didn't attend. There were counseling needs that I had to delegate. I was usually the first to leave the office. And I knew my inflexibility frustrated some people. But it was what I felt I had to do to be what my family needed me to be. I had to cheat somewhere. I decided to cheat at work. And for me, that meant cheating at church!

LEGACY

In addition to working close to home, there were two things that made this easier for me than it is for most people. First, as a pastor, I was reminded almost every week of what can happen in a marriage when husbands or wives cheat the family instead of the marketplace. I had seen mature Christian men and women fall into the trap of overinvesting at work for the sake of a big payoff down the road. Furthermore, I had seen way too many pastors sacrifice their family under the guise of doing "the Lord's work" when in fact it had little to do with the Lord's work and more to do with propping up their own egos. From the very beginning I knew what could happen if I wasn't very intentional about how I divided my time. I have never believed that I was an exception to the rule. I have all the negative potential of any other father, husband, or pastor.

The other advantage I had was growing up in the home of a successful pastor who made his family a priority. My dad was home for dinner. He never missed a basketball game (in spite of the fact that I was on the bench just about as much as he was on the bleachers). We took long family vacations. In fact, when we were on vacation we never, and I mean never, even went to church!

I could walk into his office at any moment unannounced and be warmly welcomed. I don't know how many hours a week he worked. That's really not important. What is important is that I never felt like I was competing with the church for his time. Family was clearly his priority.

These two things made it easier for me to entrust my career success to God. I have never felt the pressure some feel to build a successful church. My responsibility is to prioritize my life in accordance with the priorities laid out in Scripture. That includes doing my work as unto the Lord and loving my wife as Christ loved the church. In other words, working hard when I'm at work and then going home and forgetting about it.

In the early days, when our church was still an experiment, I had no idea how my schedule would impact progress or morale. What I did know was that we are never called to violate the principles of God in order to attain or maintain the blessings of God. I wanted to be a part of a church God would be free to bless. I really didn't know exactly what that meant. But I did know that the best way to find out was to order my private world in accordance with His priorities for me as a husband, father, and pastor.

That was more than seven years ago. I have never regretted that decision. Our children have grown out of diapers now. No one requires Sandra's constant attention. She doesn't need me to be home as early anymore. But I'm still one of the first to leave in the afternoon. And I'm almost always home for dinner. And to be honest, it is not because I am so "committed" to my family. It is because I love to go home.

I feel so strongly about this principle that I encourage our staff to follow suit. "Cheat at work," I tell 'em. "Cheat me. But don't you dare cheat at home."

MAKING A STAND

So, back to you. If you were to ask your spouse and kids what schedule changes they would love to see you make, what would they say? Maybe you should ask. Their answers may be totally impractical, but it won't hurt anything to know. Don't worry about *how*. Focus on *what*. Presume on God for a minute. Assume He is going to support you. Assume for the moment that He will come through for you, intervene on your behalf. What would your schedule look like? What would have to change?

Now before you panic, I want you to think about something. The things that will make or break you professionally are not related to the number of hours you work. A sixty-hour workweek does not guarantee you more success than a forty-five-hour workweek. Even if you are punching a clock, more hours don't result in greater success.

Think about where you are today professionally. Consider your success for just a moment. Are you where you are today as a result of the number of hours you have put in? Is there an actual correlation between the amount of hours you have worked and the success you have enjoyed? I would venture to guess that your success is the result of opportunities that came your way, lucky breaks, hunches you followed up on, people you met by accident, and risks you decided to take.

When successful men and women reminisce, their defining moments professionally are never related to how many hours they worked. And I have never heard of a business failure attributed to a work schedule. Success is always related to good decisions, unexpected opportunities, market conditions, and a host of other things that nobody really had any control over. The sixty hours you work this week may not reap nearly the same productivity as the sixty hours you put in next week. Why? Because of things you have no control over.

It is important that you associate your professional success with those things that really make a difference. And the length of your workweek does not play as significant a role as you might at first think. There are other factors that impact your success more significantly than your schedule. Again, these are things you can't control.

But the opposite is true in family life. Happily married couples never attribute their success to unexpected opportunities, market conditions, luck, or good timing. You have never met a healthy family who chalked up their success to being in the right place at the right time. With family, success is always related to *time*. In the world of family you have far more control over the things that really make a difference.

This is why it makes so much sense to entrust our careers to our Heavenly Father. For only He controls those things that make the most significant difference in our professions. This is why it is safe to ask Him to fill the gaps at work when it is time for us to go home.

Don't be afraid to consider a new schedule. Chances are, there is no necessary correlation between your current success and the number of hours you are putting in anyway. The make-or-break events, relationships, market conditions, and closings are usually related to things over which God exercises control.

So make up your mind. And then begin piecing together a plan by which you can make your decision a reality.

8

~

A FAIR TRIAL

You've made up your mind. You've identified some specific non-negotiables. You've committed to stand by your convictions. Now what? *What's the best way to get from here to there?* Specifically, how do you go about convincing your employer to lighten up?

In short, very carefully.

Building up a head of steam over your decision to reprioritize could be dangerous. The goal in this exercise is not to lose your job or even to make a point with the folks in your office. The goal is to negotiate your way into a more manageable and flexible schedule. Once again, Daniel provides us with a model to follow. Daniel knew how to be both dogmatic and diplomatic, which is not always an easy thing to do. He was not going to compromise his convictions. But he was not going to demand his way either.

It would have been easy for Daniel to take a defiant posture with the Babylonians. But Daniel resisted. He didn't stage a hunger strike or withdraw into passive-aggressive resistance of their authority. Daniel was committed to doing the right thing, the right way. He was dogmatic in his convictions, but not in his approach. He was immovable yet humble, unshakable but sensitive.

WISDOM AND TACT

This unusual ability to maintain his cool in a highly emotional environment surfaces again later in Daniel's tenure under Nebuchadnezzar. Years later the king has a dream that he expects his wise men to recount for him and interpret. Interpreting dreams was one thing. Telling the king what he dreamed was something else entirely. The king loses his patience and decides to execute his entire staff of wise men and magicians. When Daniel hears of the king's edict, he sets out to find the commander in charge of carrying out the king's orders. Notice Daniel's approach:

> When Arioch, the commander of the king's guard, had gone out to put to death the wise men of Babylon, Daniel spoke to him with *wisdom* and *tact*. (Daniel 2:14, emphasis mine)

"Wisdom and tact." He is hours, perhaps minutes, away from losing his life over something he had nothing to do with, and he is able to approach the commander with wisdom and tact. Desperation and fear I could understand, but not wisdom and tact.

Now before you write Daniel off as just another larger-than-life Bible superhero, you need to know something else about this story. After Daniel's diplomatic discussion with Arioch, he went home and had a different kind of discussion with his buddies.

Here's what happened:

> Then Daniel returned to his house and explained the matter to his friends Hananiah, Mishael and Azariah. He urged them to plead for mercy from the God of heaven concerning this mystery, so that he and his friends might not be executed with the rest of the wise men of Babylon. (Daniel 2:17–18)

Daniel was not completely fearless. He didn't have a death wish. He was not above begging God for mercy. He knew that tact and diplomacy were not enough to get them over this hurdle. They were going to need another "now God" moment to survive.

So what's the lesson in all of this?

God honors diplomacy and dependency. One doesn't supplant the other. Both are necessary. Having a plan isn't a lack of faith. Walking in and giving an ultimatum at work isn't necessarily an expression of faith. You need wisdom, tact, and some friends praying for you back at home.

POSTURING

I belabor this point because I know firsthand how easy it is for the pendulum to swing from one extreme to the other. When we at last catch a glimpse of the hurt we have caused at home, there is something in us that wants to fix things immediately. It is not enough to make up our minds; we want to do something.

But the wrong actions for the right reason produce painful results. You can do the right thing the wrong way and end up in a worse situation than the one you left. The operative word throughout this book has been *choosing,* not *reacting.*

The fact that you have decided to make a change in your life does not necessarily mean the folks at work are under any obligation to change. There is no value in punishing your employer. Your attitude and approach should be seasoned with diplomacy and tact. Besides, the source of your frustration is not your employer. It is the decisions you have made in response to the demands of your employer and the marketplace in general. Nobody forced you to work there. It was your decision. You, not they, must bear the consequences.

CHEATING AND DECEIVING

One other point of clarification needs to be made at this point. Cheating at work has nothing to do with cheating your employer. As we pointed out in the introduction, cheating in this context is about reallocating your limited time assets according to your predetermined priorities. Cheating at work has nothing to do with deceiving your employer. As we have said on several occasions, the blessings of God are never attained by violating the principles of God. Daniel didn't secretly abandon the king's diet plan. There was no deceit. He told the official exactly what his intentions were. Then he prepared himself for the consequences.

Depending on your job situation, this approach may call for a great deal of candor with your employer. The more nonconfrontational your personality, the more difficult it will be for you to actually approach your boss or supervisor with whatever plan you come up with. You may be tempted to simply start cutting out early, leaving her with a false impression, living with the hopes that she doesn't discover that you aren't around as much. But that's not what we are suggesting.

THE PLAN

Buried in the interaction between Daniel and the king's official is the framework for a transition strategy that can be lifted out of its original context and applied in our modern culture.

For the remainder of this chapter, we will examine the three components that serve as the outline for Daniel's course of action. If you work for yourself or are in a position where you set your own hours, steps one and two may not be relevant for your situation. But don't skip the third step.

I really don't like lists. Life doesn't happen according to any list I have ever read. And I have never mastered anything by following a list. Furthermore, I don't think Daniel was following a prescribed method in his attempt to broker a deal with the king's official. So, I don't view these three elements as a prescription that must be followed. But as you think through how you will approach those in authority over you at the office, you would do well to consider Daniel's strategy.

Essentially, Daniel did three things:

1. He asked for permission to change his work conditions.

2. He listened to the objections from his supervisor.

3. He proposed a test that took into account his supervisor's concerns.

DANIEL ASKED

[A]nd he [Daniel] asked the chief official for permission not to defile himself in this way. (Daniel 1:8)

The first thing Daniel did was go right to the person in charge and address the issue head-on. He didn't attempt to deceive the king's official. He didn't stage a hunger strike. He went right up and asked to be an exception to the rule.

He didn't demand. He asked. He didn't ask with the assumption that his personal conviction would carry any weight with the king's official. What was imperative for him was certainly not imperative for everyone else. In addition, Daniel offered an alternative. He didn't simply tell the king's official what he didn't want to eat. He suggested a substitute diet.

If you are in a position where you are not free to adjust your schedule without running it by someone first, Daniel's approach has a lot of merit.

- Address the issue directly.

- Ask, don't demand.

- Offer alternatives.

When I challenge men and women to address this issue with their supervisors, I receive varying responses, everything from "She will probably understand," to "He's liable to let me go right then and there." Chances are, your anticipated response falls somewhere between those two. If you don't expect to get much support from your boss or supervisor, you may be tempted to avoid this step altogether. That would probably be a big mistake.

Addressing the issue directly accomplishes three things. It allows you to discover how serious you are about your decision. It gives you an opportunity to find out if you are operating under false assumptions about your employer. Your boss may be more open than you suspect. Most important, addressing the issue directly gives your Heavenly Father an opportunity to work on your behalf. If you choose not to address your schedule directly, you may be inclined to cheat your employer. Being direct will help you avoid the temptation to be deceitful.

Ask; don't demand. Even if you are ready to walk, just ask. When we ask, we underscore our supervisor's authority. When we demand, we undermine his or her authority.

Don't include an ultimatum with your request. An ultimatum will put your supervisor on the defensive. It is very important for bosses to feel like they are making a decision rather than responding to a threat. People will knowingly make a bad decision just to save face when they are threatened.

Offer alternatives. You can anticipate what some of the concerns will be. You know some of what your supervisor will feel like he or she is giving up by allowing you to adjust your schedule. Address those losses. Chances are, if your boss knows you have thought the issue through from his perspective, he will not feel as if he has to defend anything. Do your best to give back more than you are taking away.

If the answer is "no," just thank the boss for her time and go back to work. Now is not the time to communicate your inflexibility on this issue. Wait. Give God an opportunity to work. As an employer, I know there have been many occasions that I have said "no" to a request and then changed my mind the next day, once I had an opportunity to think about it.

DANIEL LISTENED

> [T]he commander of the officials said to Daniel, "I am afraid of my lord the king, who has appointed your food and your drink; for why should he see your faces looking more haggard than the youths who are your own age? Then you would make me forfeit my head to the king." (Daniel 1:9–10)

Once Daniel had taken his idea public, he *listened*. And when he did, he discovered some extremely valuable information. He found out that the king's official was open to altering the meal plan. The issue was not what Daniel ate; it was how he looked and performed. So Daniel went to work on addressing the official's primary concern. We'll return to this topic later.

Chances are, you are pretty confident you know what your employer's concerns will be. But of the three or four things mentioned, most likely, one of them will be her chief concern. Listen with the goal of identifying the issue that makes your supervisor most uncomfortable with your proposal. Where exactly do the fingernails hit the chalkboard?

Don't argue. Don't confront. Ask lots of questions. Ask for clarification. Dig. Discover. Empathize. Take notes. Nod. Agree. And then leave! If possible, leave before you hear "no." When all the issues are on the table and you think you may have a bead on the one or two primary concerns, get up and go. End the conversation with something along the lines of, "I see how this request might cause a problem. If I were you, I would be concerned about that (once you have discerned what "that" is) as well. The last thing I want to do is hurt the company or embarrass you in any way. If it is all right with you, I would like to think about what you have said and get back with you."

If the answer wasn't "yes" you have to go back, so do what you can to keep the door cracked.

DANIEL PROPOSED A TEST

But Daniel said to the overseer . . . "Please test your servants for ten days . . . Then let our appearance be observed in your presence, and the appearance of the youths who are eating the king's choice food; and deal with your servants according to what you see (Daniel 1:11–13)."

Once Daniel identified the official's chief concern, he went back and proposed a test. Since performance rather than diet was the issue, he figured the thing to do was to challenge the king's official to scrutinize his performance.

Notice how he closes his proposal:

[A]nd deal with your servants according to what you see.

Once again, he never threatened the official's authority or control. Still, there was no ultimatum. By committing to a ten-day trial, Daniel's overseer had virtually little to lose. How sick could Daniel become in just ten days? Certainly any sign of diet-related frailty in such a short period could be easily reversed. Furthermore, it's assumed that he could have stopped the experiment at just one or two days if he changed his mind.

Here's where you have something in common with Daniel. His overseer's primary concern was performance, not diet. That is your employer's primary concern as well. The real issue is not the number of hours we spend in the office; it is productivity that matters. Without knowing what you do for a living, I would wager that there are several factors that affect your productivity as much as, or more than, time. Knowing what these are works to your advantage.

The next step for you, whether you report directly to someone else or not, is to set up a trial. A trial is disarming. If anyone has objections, a well-designed trial will usually isolate those concerns and neutralize them. How much can go wrong in two or three weeks? Besides, you are inviting your boss to scrutinize your productivity. How many people have walked into his office in the past six months and asked for closer supervision and additional evaluation?

A trial is not a compromise. It is not a watered-down version of your original conviction. Daniel didn't compromise his standard. He devised a way for the king's official to see first-hand that he could alter his diet without reducing his productivity. The test was merely a tool through which to demonstrate his point.

You see, cheating at work isn't really cheating at all. It's merely testing to see how well the requirements of your job can be met under a different arrangement. Odds are, your performance will improve. I say that based on the testimonies of those who have taken this challenge. What is initially viewed as a self-serving concession that benefits only you may in fact turn out to benefit the entire company.

I mentioned earlier that if you are in control of your schedule, you should seriously consider making this step. Set up a trial. Tell your family what you intend to do. Establish an objective way to measure your productivity. Set a time limit, preferably thirty days, and stick with your schedule. Come home on time. Limit your travel.

This is far more effective than telling yourself, "I'm going to do better."

You will be far more motivated to be consistent for a pre-scribed period of time than you will if you make a commit-ment to change forever. Instead of a "from now on" promise, just make a "for the next thirty days" promise. That's measur-able. That's something you can stay focused on.

You need to do this for your sake. You need to see what God is willing to do on your behalf if you will simply trust Him. When you do a trial, you will be watching with greater intensity. You will pay better attention to detail. You will know if it is working.

THE INTERVENTION

And at the end of ten days their appearance seemed better and they were fatter than all the youths who had been eating the king's choice food. So the overseer continued to with-hold their choice food and the wine they were to drink, and kept giving them vegetables. And as for these four youths, God gave them knowledge and intelligence in every branch of literature and wisdom; Daniel even understood all kinds of visions and dreams. (Daniel 1:15–17)

One can't help but wonder what Daniel would have done if the test had not gone in his favor. Was there a plan B? Would Daniel have proposed a different test? Would he have appealed directly to the king?

We don't know.

But every indication is that Daniel had no intention of

shrinking from his original decision. He would remain committed to his priorities, regardless of the outcome of the trial. But don't you know he was doing everything in his power to outperform his peers during those critical ten days! And it worked. His alternative diet enhanced his performance.

The text, however, indicates that something divine happened. Daniel and his friends didn't merely outsmart their peers. There weren't simply the benefactors of a healthy diet. Verse 17 says, "God gave them knowledge and intelligence." They were the recipients of divine intervention. Not a miracle per se, there was nothing observably supernatural about what happened, but there was certainly something special about those Israelite boys.

Through the years I have challenged hundreds of men and women to follow Daniel's example. Again and again those who have taken me up on the challenge come back with remarkable stories to tell. Stories that often border on the supernatural events that hint of divine intervention:

"I get more work done in less time."

"An opportunity dropped in my lap out of nowhere."

"A deal I assumed was dead suddenly sprang back to life."

"I have more business than I can keep up with."

And that's just on the business side. On the domestic front things are always better as well. Men, especially, talk about how much more they enjoy going home. As one fellow expressed it, "I feel like my wife is actually happy to see me."

You'll never know what God is willing to do on your behalf until you are willing to step out and to trust Him. When your obedience intersects with His faithfulness, you will sense His divine presence. You will experience the intervention of the Father.

God honors those who honor Him. Honor Him at home and experience His blessing there. Honor Him in the marketplace and look for Him to show up there as well.

God is not a stranger to the marketplace. He created economics. He understands values. There are more verses in the Bible about money than about heaven and hell combined. He is as capable of intervening in your office on Monday afternoon as He is in your church on Sunday morning. Because your work is important to you, it is important to Him— because you are important to Him.

Position yourself to be blessed by conducting your business in a way that invites God into the mix. Determine a schedule that honors your employer and your family. If necessary, present your ideas to your boss. Conduct a trial. And then watch to see what God does on your behalf.

9

⌐

TRADING PLACES

In the real world there are few fairy tale endings. This whole process may continue to seem out of reach from where you sit. Even Daniel's story may be a little too "and they all lived happily ever after" for you. That's understandable. In a highly competitive market the odds are against you being cut much slack. So it seemed appropriate to end our time together with a story about a friend of mine who got "no" for an answer.

I have known Grant for fifteen years. He has been a mentor as well as a friend. Grant is fifty-eight and has four incredible kids, and eight fine grandkids, and a marriage that most couples would die for. Early in our friendship I asked Grant to tell me how he ended up working for himself. The story that followed is one that I have told many times. And it has given me courage at several critical junctions in my own journey.

When he was in his early twenties, Grant went to work for a fellow in the outdoor advertising business. Basically, they built and sold advertisements on billboards. Now Grant is the kind of guy who could sell just about anything to anybody. So he did quite well in the outdoor advertising business. One thing led to another, and before long Grant was making a lot of money for a kid his age. Furthermore, the owner, Tom, promised Grant a cut of the profits if he ever sold the business, which he eventually did. But there was a problem.

Tom expected his employees to work six days a week. He lived for his business, and he figured everybody else ought to as well. If you weren't in the office Monday through Saturday, there was something wrong. You weren't a company man. Whenever anyone in the inner circle griped, he reminded him or her of the big payoff down the road.

Now Grant didn't mind working hard. And he certainly didn't mind being well compensated for his labor. But he and Patty and at that time his two "young-uns," as he referred to them, didn't see eye to eye with Tom when it came to prioritizing business and family. Grant and Patty had a vision for their family that went beyond owning a big house and a couple of new cars. And working every Saturday pretty much eliminated any hopes they had of creating the family environment they were envisioning.

So Grant made up his mind to forgo this "excellent" opportunity. As he tells the story, "Me and Patty sat down and decided that this was not the way we were going to raise our family. So I decided to offer Tom an alternative schedule and if he couldn't accept that, we would just have to find something else to do."

As it turned out, Tom was not open to Grant's suggestion. But as Grant found out later, Tom didn't think he had the nerve just to walk out. When Grant turned in his resignation, Tom grinned and asked Grant what he was going to do. Grant told him he didn't know—and he didn't. But he knew one thing: whatever he found to do next, it would *support* rather than compete with what he envisioned for his family. In Grant's words, "I told Tom I would let him determine my exit strategy and that I would do everything I could to insure a smooth transition. I don't think he thought I was serious. He knew I couldn't go anywhere else and make that kind of money. And I wasn't sure I could either." So after a couple of awkward weeks in the office, Grant and Patty loaded up the station wagon with everything they could carry and headed out of town.

Now I'm tempted not to tell you the rest of the story. The reason being, it is really not important. The point is, Grant decided to quit cheating at home. And now, these many years later, he looks back at that decision and considers it a defining moment, not so much in terms of his career, but in terms of what happened to his family. Grant didn't know what would happen financially. But he knew what he could not continue to allow this to happen in his family.

Grant went on to begin his own outdoor company in a different part of the country. God blessed his courage and commitment. His businesses have thrived. But more important, he and his wife saw their vision for their children become a reality.

As I mentioned, his former employer did finally sell his

company. The men who stayed with him all those years received big checks. But most of them had lost their families along the way. A couple of them declared bankruptcy a few years after they received their compensation. The owner of the company paid a price relationally as well. His children are grown and gone. His interaction with them is infrequent and superficial.

Looking back, Grant has no doubt that God intervened on his behalf. "My conviction about working six days a week was the thing God used to get us out of that situation," he said. This was his "now God" moment. It wasn't a miracle in the supernatural sense. But it was clearly God's tangible faithfulness in the life of a couple who was committed to doing things right.

THE REST OF THE STORY

In Chapter 1, I introduced you to Bill. He experienced a "now God" moment as well.

When we left off, Bill had just made up his mind to stop cheating at home. He sat down with his wife, Carol, and identified several non-negotiables. He would limit travel to one night a week—a criteria that seemed unrealistic if he was going to function as a CEO. In addition, they established a weekly date night. Bill determined to be home in time to put his daughters to bed each night. And he would stop working on Sundays.

As Bill reviewed the changes he would need to make, it became apparent that he was going to need to make a job change. He knew it was pointless to even discuss these kinds of issues with his current employer. His only option was to start looking for another opportunity.

Because of his background and education, Bill was confident that he could find another job. The challenge would be finding a company that would allow him the flexibility he needed in order to accomplish what he desperately needed to accomplish at home.

A few days after he had determined to make a change, Bill received a call from an old friend. Jim, a Christian, was the owner of a small entertainment company in Atlanta. Bill had served on its board in the past but had never considered the company a prospect for his own employment. The entertainment industry wasn't even on his radar at this time. When Jim asked how things were going, it was as if he opened a floodgate. As Bill shared the details of his dilemma, the tears began to flow. Jim listened as Bill described the changes he needed to make and the challenge of finding employment that would afford him that kind of flexibility.

Then Jim said something that Bill never expected: "Well, it is funny you mentioned that. As you know I'm retiring in November. The purpose of my call was to see if you would be open to serving as chairman of our company. I've hesitated for some time to contact you about this because frankly, I just didn't think this would be something you would be open to."

As Jim began to describe the job, it sounded like the perfect solution. The company was domestic, not international. It was private, not public. Travel would be limited.

There was just one problem. The salary was about 30 percent below what Bill needed in order to reach his financial goals.

But God wasn't finished yet.

Jim suggested they pray together right there on the phone. By now, Bill was in his parking space at work. So he listened while Jim asked God to give Bill something part-time to help bridge the gap to allow Bill to make the job change. Jim specifically asked God for something like a board seat with a company that would pay the extra 30 percent.

Bill hung up the phone, walked into his office, and sat down at the desk to start his day. Just then, the phone rang. It was a recruiter wanting to know if Bill might be interested in a board seat for a company based in Memphis. The pay was almost exactly the 30 percent Bill needed to bridge the gap. "I'd never had anything like that happen in my life! It sent chills up my spine. I called Carol, and we both cried as we reflected on God's faithfulness to our family."

Within a couple of months Bill had made the transition. "For the first time in years, I have peace in my life. My marriage is healthier. My kids are happier. I have renewed my friendships. I don't have to miss church. Things are better than they have ever been."

ALL IN A DAY'S WORK

Bill and Grant's stories are not as unusual as you might think. I don't believe for a minute that God guarantees us a salary upgrade if we obey Him. But I do know that God honors those who place their faith in Him. Jesus summarized it this way:

> But seek first His kingdom and His righteousness; and all these things shall be added to you. (Matthew 6:33 NASB)

In other words, order your world around your Heavenly Father's priorities for you and then trust Him to fill the gaps created by your faithfulness. Instead of asking God to stand watch over your family while you give to your career what belongs at home, turn the prayer around. Go home, seek Him first, and ask Him to watch over things at work. In time, you will discover that when you prioritize correctly at work and home, God will honor you in *both* arenas. Everybody wins.

MISPLACED LOYALTY

Let's face it. One day you will come home from the office for the last time. Nobody retires from his or her family to spend his or her final days in the office. Your last day may be at sixty-five when you retire or at thirty-five when you are laid off. Either way, you are coming home. What and who you come home to will be determined by what and who you choose to cheat between now and then.

If you are like most, one person stands between you and the end of your current employment. Tomorrow, you could be called in to someone's office and told that your services are not needed anymore. Perhaps a decision like that would require the vote of a board. Either way, somebody has the power to send you home with the contents of your office in the trunk of your car.

I have seen too many men and women cheat their family only to find that the companies they worked for were not nearly as loyal to them as they were to the companies.

Loyalty in the marketplace is rarely reciprocated. It is sad when a man or woman is forced out of an organization they bled for to return home to the family they have neglected.

Why give your ultimate loyalty to an organization where your value is conditioned upon your ability to perform? Why betray those whose loyalty is unconditional? Why devote so much of yourself to something you know you will leave, and so little time to those you will eventually come home to? It doesn't make any sense, does it? Yet without a conscious decision to do otherwise, that is exactly what most of us are prone to do.

THE THIRTY-DAY CHALLENGE

In closing, I want to urge you to take the thirty-day challenge. Make up your mind not to cheat at home for thirty days. Mark it on your calendar. Sit down with your spouse and determine exactly what that will look like. And then start!

Instead of leaving the office when you are finished with everything, leave in time to get home when you have committed to be home. For thirty days say "no" to anything that has the potential to pull you away from your decision.

Decide now to say "no" at those times. In doing so you place your career and finances squarely in the capable hands of your heavenly Father.

As you drive away from the office, ask for God to fill the gaps at the office while you attend to your unique responsibilities at home. At the end of thirty days, sit down and evaluate what has happened at home, your finances, and your productivity at work. You will be surprised.

Everybody cheats. Don't cheat the people who love you most. Don't cheat the person who is looking forward to spending the rest of his or her life with you. Don't cheat yourself of the peace that comes with knowing that you are squarely in the will of the One who created you. Don't cheat your kids of the security that comes with knowing that they are Mommy and Daddy's priority.

It has been said before. It is worth saying again. Nobody gets to the end of his life and wishes he had spent more time at the office. You won't be the first.

Make up your mind.

Develop a plan.

Deliver it diplomatically.

Be willing to walk.

And then watch for God.

After all, He takes full responsibility for the life that is wholly devoted to Him.

ABOUT THE AUTHOR

Andy Stanley serves as senior pastor of North Point Community Church in north Atlanta. He received his master of theology degree from Dallas Theological Seminary. He is the author of *Like a Rock* (Thomas Nelson) and *Visioneeering* (Multnomah), and the co-author of *The Seven Checkpoints for Students* (Howard) and *Can We Do That?* (Howard). He and his wife, Sandra, are the parents of three children.

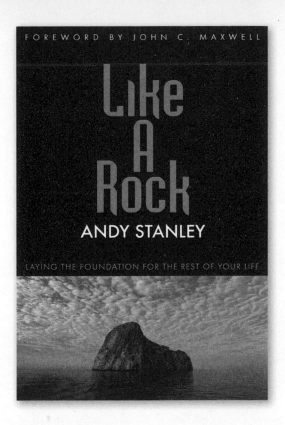

FOREWORD BY JOHN C. MAXWELL

Like A Rock

ANDY STANLEY

LAYING THE FOUNDATION FOR THE REST OF YOUR LIFE

Each person's character is either developing or deteriorating. Only those who intentionally pursue character development are moving toward their goals for who they hope to be. This book presents a step-by-step plan for overcoming the negative inertia of this fallen world to move forward toward success.

ISBN 0-7852-6579-1

For an audio version of

Choosing To Cheat

as presented on a Sunday morning at

North Point Community Church,

as well as other resources by Andy Stanley,

please visit the

North Point Resources

web site at

www.northpoint.org,

call (770)290-5621

or write

North Point Resources
4350 North Point Parkway
Alpharetta, GA 30022